Copyright © 2019 Pete Alexander
All rights reserved. No part of this book may be used or reproduced in any manner whatsoever without prior written consent of the authors, except as provided by the United States of America copyright law.

Published by Best Seller Publishing®, Pasadena, CA
Best Seller Publishing® is a registered trademark
Printed in the United States of America.
ISBN 978-1-072704-99-7

This publication is designed to provide accurate and authoritative information with regard to the subject matter covered. It is sold with the understanding that the publisher is not engaged in rendering health, wellness, or medical advice. If legal advice or other expert assistance is required, the services of a competent professional should be sought. The opinions expressed by the authors in this book are not endorsed by Best Seller Publishing® and are the sole responsibility of the author rendering the opinion.

Most Best Seller Publishing® titles are available at special quantity discounts for bulk purchases for sales promotions, premiums, fundraising, and educational use. Special versions or book excerpts can also be created to fit specific needs.

For more information, please write:
Best Seller Publishing®
1346 Walnut Street, #205
Pasadena, CA 91106
or call 1(626) 765 9750
Toll Free: 1(844) 850-3500
Visit us online at: www.BestSellerPublishing.org

Dedication

For Olga, Anthony, and Beverly. Thank you for all your support and encouragement as I follow my path.

About the Author

As the old saying goes, "shit happens." Including a dysfunctional childhood, rocky relationships, divorce, or suicidal family members, my life has seen its ups and downs. My personal growth path has been an amazing journey, and I am grateful for everything I currently have. I am also grateful for the personal success I have experienced professionally.

During my career, I have had the privilege to work in a variety of sales and marketing roles. Each role had one thing in common: high stress. It got to the point that I was diagnosed with stress-related diabetes and also ended up in the hospital with a severe case of diabetic ketoacidosis, a few hours away from being comatose.

It was a reality check for me. When you don't have your health, not much else matters. I knew it was time for me to walk away, even though I had a great job, secure income, and good benefits. Interestingly, my coworkers and peers were very supportive; many of them even told me they admired my decision to put my health first before my career because they were contemplating the same thing. I realized then that it wasn't just me, and now I have dedicated my professional career to helping other sales and marketing professionals avoid my mistakes and benefit from the wonderful tools and techniques I have learned and experienced firsthand.

Please note that while the techniques in this book have produced remarkable results for others, there is no guarantee a particular stress-relief tool will work for you. Thus, you must take complete responsibility for using them and for your own physical and emotional wellbeing. **Further, I am not a licensed health professional**. Please consult qualified health practitioners regarding your use of any of these techniques. Medical advice must only be obtained from a physician or qualified health practitioner.

Contents

Preface

Stress is all around us—at work, at home, online ... you name it. A simple Google search on stress will pull up over one billion results on what stress is, types of it, what causes it, symptoms, and what you can do about it. But we don't need Google to tell us if we're stressed: the reality is, we know it because our mind and body are delivering clear signals that we are taxing ourselves. The problem is that we don't have the time to figure out how to deal with stress in the now, and then we stress out about not being able to deal with our stress: a vicious circle.

Sure, you could buy a book or download an app on meditating, or breathing, or journaling, or exercising. You could open the book or app and give it a try, but it probably didn't work. Why? Maybe you didn't give it enough time. Maybe you tried it while also responding to 100 emails. Maybe the techniques provided were too complicated or time-intensive, so now you're frustrated and thinking "I've got this really important meeting/presentation this morning, where I have to be at my best. Isn't there some tool or technique that can help me right now, in this moment?"

The answer is yes! If you flip through this book you will see that there are hundreds of fast, effective, and easy tips and tools designed specifically to be used in the now. Why so many? Because you are unique, so there is no such thing as a one-size fits all tool for stress relief. What works for one person may not work for someone else.

The book's foundation is the LIGHTEN™ Model, and the tools suggested are organized around the areas of your life that need to be nurtured in order to achieve long-term stress relief: Livelihood (career), Imagination, Genius (unconscious mind), Health, Time, Environment, and Network (relationships). If you are stressed about hitting your sales quota, take a look at the Livelihood or Time chapter. Worried about that next presentation? The Imagination chapter has some great techniques. Anxious about your next doctor's appointment? Check out the Genius or Health chapter. Meeting your in-laws? The Network chapter is the place to go.

The intent of this book is that you keep it handy for whenever or wherever you need it: that important meeting/presentation, that difficult conversation you need to have, the multiple priorities all needing your attention right now, or anything else that stresses you out when shit happens.

If you just have a couple minutes to spare to get some quick-and-easy stress relief, this book is for you.

Why I Fought Back Against Stress

When a person goes into the operating room, he realizes that there is one book that he has yet to finish reading, "The Book of Healthy Life."

—STEVE JOBS, COFOUNDER AND FORMER CEO,
APPLE INC.

I wrote this book because stress almost killed me—literally.

Over 35 years, I have had the privilege of being a salesperson, marketing professional, professor, and business owner,[1] but each role had one thing in common: high stress. As a salesperson, I had the monthly, quarterly, and annual stress of reaching and exceeding my quota. As a marketing professional, I had to deal with unrealistic project deadlines and minimal budget and resources. There were also the senior executives who felt it was their job to criticize the littlest things when it came to our department's deliverables.

As a professor, I needed to stay on top of frequently changing digital marketing trends. I also had to manage the needs of demanding students, and review their work fairly and deliver grade reports on short timelines.

Finally, as a small business owner, I had to serve as everything from president to janitor. It was up to me to ensure economic prosperity so that my employees and vendors got paid and the business could grow.

In each role I held, I was a workaholic, typically working more than 60 hours per week. In parallel, I chose to be married at 29, become a father at 31 and 35, and earn a PhD in business administration at 41: a classic stressed-out multitasker if ever there was one.

My multitasking prowess didn't prepare me for the perfect storm of stressful events in 2008, including my father passing and my strained marriage on its way to a divorce. At that time, during the Great Recession, I ran a landscaping business that needed my constant attention, while my children expected me to be present and available at a moment's notice.

Under the load of the stress, my body started breaking down. First, my back locked up to the point that I couldn't sit or stand comfortably. Then, my knees got a severe case of bursitis, causing stiffness and pain when I walked. Last but certainly not least, I was diagnosed with stress-induced diabetes.

I always thought that diabetes was a disease for overweight and/or sedentary people, yet I was the complete opposite of that. Furthermore, only one of my cousins had diabetes, so my genes had nothing to do with it either. Nevertheless, I had it. I was prescribed various forms of insulin and medical supplies to deal with this disease.

Several years later, my blood sugars began to rise, and I had to take more and more insulin to compensate. What I discovered was that my body was becoming insulin-resistant, and I now had to take another drug just to get my body to absorb more of the synthetic insulin I was taking. When you have to take one drug to make another drug more effective, you know you are on a slippery slope.

What I hadn't noticed at the time was the direct correlation between my stress level and my glucose numbers. Usually, I aim for a range of 80-120mg/dl. If I'm not stressed, I'm typically in this range. When I am stressed, my numbers are typically between 165-225mg/dl, or higher under extreme stress. I finally realized that my body was telling me I needed to calm down.

Yet I didn't listen to my body. I was too busy with other things in life: kids, career, new relationship, volunteer work, you name it. I was taking care of other important things without first taking care of my health. And I knew better. Like clockwork, when I ran myself at full speed for too long, I would inevitably come crashing down. This would result in the flu, a sinus infection, or something similar, and I would be left bedridden and wishing I had better health.

Ten years later, my real wakeup call came.

My Epiphany

I was working long hours, including nights and weekends, trying to keep a very important and high-profile project on track. I was stress eating (meaning grab-and-go high-carb food), not sleeping well, and worrying about everything, like I normally did. One Sunday, my fiancé (now my wife) Olga and I went to lunch, and I immediately got light-headed. I couldn't eat anything because my stomach felt like it was having a bad case of heartburn. Olga took me to a nearby fire station, where they hooked me up to an EKG machine and blood pressure monitor. My heart vital signs looked okay, but they recommended I check into the local emergency room (ER). I thought it was only heartburn because a few decades before, I had ended up in a Las Vegas ER with heartburn and food poisoning, which I had picked up at a questionable roadside diner.

Rather than heading to the ER, we stopped at the pharmacy for anti-heartburn medicine. It didn't do anything for me, so I went to lie down. I barely remember what happened next. I later learned that Olga saw me turning green, and she gave me the choice: get in the car so she could take me to the ER, or she was going to call an ambulance. Either way, I was going to the hospital.

Lucky for me she had insisted. I was admitted immediately (I must have looked terrible), and more than three liters of fluids were given to me intravenously. I was then transferred to the intensive care unit (ICU) with a severe case of diabetic ketoacidosis. My body was eating away at my muscles and there was a ton of acid in my blood. No wonder the feeling in my stomach felt like heartburn. The doctor said that had I not come in when I did, I would have ended up in a coma within a few hours.

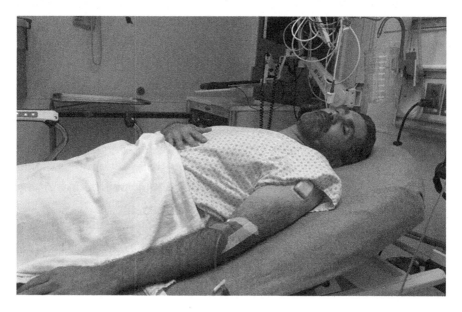

In the emergency room with a severe case of diabetic ketoacidosis.

Of course, as a dedicated employee, I notified my boss that I was in the hospital. At about 6:00 a.m. the next morning I received a text from my boss asking me what I was going to do about the webinar I was supposed to run at 8:00 a.m. I immediately jumped into fix-it mode. I pushed the limits of my smart phone while I tried to reschedule the webinar to another day, since I knew that my doctor and nurses would not let me go through with the webinar as planned.

I noticed immediately that my glucose numbers started to skyrocket, and that's when I had my epiphany. My insulin was only treating the symptom of the problem (high glucose), but I needed to treat the source of the problem, which was the negative stress that had caused such a catastrophic reaction in my body.

During my time in ICU, I was able to reflect on the journey that had led me to this unhealthy state. After a lifelong struggle with stress that I had never truly dealt with, it was no surprise that my body finally failed me. The surprising part was that it took over 40 years to happen.

You see, stress and I have had a long history together, dating back to my childhood growing up in an alcoholic and dysfunctional household. Lowlights include my parents divorcing when I was seven, multiple marriages for both parents after that (nine in total), and abusive alcoholic stepfathers. I had to move to new schools frequently (three just in fifth grade), and I lived in households where income was often low and food wasn't always sufficient because it was second to my parents' need for booze and cigarettes.

As a 13-year-old, I was seduced by a 46-year-old family friend. At 14, I had suicidal tendencies because of my environment. Early in my 20s, I had the misfortune of returning home one afternoon to find that my stepfather had hanged himself. What a tumultuous childhood it was. To survive that stressful environment required me to abandon being a "regular kid" and behave like an adult well before time.

I was fortunate to find a 12-step program called Adult Children of Alcoholic and Dysfunctional Families (ACoA) that taught me how to become my own loving parent. When I started the program, I felt like I was a 60-year-old in a 25-year-old body. Soon, that aging started to reverse as I learned to first like myself, and then love myself.

I am convinced that ACoA saved my life, and I have stayed active in the program sponsoring and coaching others dealing with stress since the early 1990s. In 2012, my community asked me to go on stage to talk about my childhood experience with a presentation titled "Break The Cycle of Family Dysfunction,"[2] and I continue to speak at various meetings sharing my story of hope and recovery.

What I Did After My Epiphany

Lying in bed throughout my first extended hospital stay was not only an epiphany moment but also a reality check. I realized that when you don't have your health, not much else matters.

I knew it was time for me to seriously start applying stress relief tools. So, I did. Friends, family, and coworkers noticed immediately that I was a different person. I was calm, collected, and focused on my vision that stress was no longer going to get the best of me.

I decided to walk away from the corporate world, even though I had a great job, secure income, and good benefits. Interestingly, my coworkers and peers were very supportive and the majority of them told me they admired my decision to put my health before my career. Some of them told me in confidence that they were jealous and wished they could do the same. Inspired by this knowledge, I transformed my career to help other professionals avoid my mistakes by benefiting from the wonderful tools and techniques I have learned and experienced firsthand.

In addition to writing this book, I have a thriving coaching practice where I help working professionals overcome their obstacles and barriers to success that are causing them stress. I present at various conferences and meetings where I facilitate breakout sessions on stress relief. I also have a blog where I post weekly video instructions on stress relief tools that you can subscribe to at **PeteAlexander.com**.

I am truly blessed to have aligned my health, knowledge, and passion around this critical subject.

How This Book Will Help You

Unlike most stress-related self-help books on the market, this one gets right to the point so that you can take action. However, there is some context needed, so the next chapter gives you research and background on what stress may be doing to you, and it is followed by a chapter describing my proprietary and foundational LIGHTEN™ Model for stress relief. These chapters provide a deeper look into stress in general and the philosophy of balancing the different components of one's life as well.

After that, it's all about you. The book is smartly organized into seven chapters full of tips, suggestions, and techniques that fit into the timeframe you have (shortest to longest, starting with activities requiring only one minute) and the areas of your life where long-term stress manifests: Livelihood (career), Imagination (active mind), Genius (unconscious mind), Health, Time, Environment, and Network (relationships).

All of the tools included in this book have a short introduction explaining the tool and why it is important. However, to streamline your experience even more, each tool gives you the ability to get right to the activity: simply look for the boxes titled "Lighten Your Day."

I hope you get as much benefit from the tools in this book as I have. Congratulations on taking your first step to stress relief!

Don't let your mind bully your body into believing it must carry the burden of its worries.

—ASTRID ALAUDA (PEN NAME OF TERRI GUILLEMETS),
AMERICAN ANTHOLOGIST AND AUTHOR

CHAPTER 1

What's Stress Costing You?

*If you ask what is the single most important key
to longevity, I would have to say it is avoiding
worry, stress and tension. And if you didn't ask
me, I'd still have to say it.*

—GEORGE BURNS, AMERICAN COMEDIAN

Ken and I were friends for over 30 years. We met in high school
when I was 16 and formed a strong bond trying to repair my
piece-of-crap first car, a 1969 Mercury Monterrey two-door
hardtop. We nicknamed it "The Merc," and it was a beast: 26-feet long,
each door was six feet long, and it got a whopping four miles to the gallon
in fuel economy. We got into a car accident the week after school let out
and spent the entire summer break trying to repair it.

That experience made us inseparable. People referred to us as Laurel
and Hardy because Ken was short and blond, and I was taller and dark
haired. Our personalities were also similar to that famous comedy duo.
After high school, our friendship remained intact, and we served as each
other's best man at our weddings, as well as supporting each other as we
became proud fathers.

Fast forward 20 years. Ken was struggling in his career and relationships, and I noticed that his stress was mounting. He told me he felt like a failure because he was out of work, which made him feel unworthy in his relationship with his significant other.

We would have long talks during which I would try to encourage him to not stress as much. He humored me by saying he would try a couple tools that I told him had worked for me, but I knew he was just saying that to appease me. If only he had even tried one or two stress relief techniques, things might have been different. More on that later in this chapter.

What the Research Says About Stress

Ken's story of stress is not uncommon. I've come across some eye-opening statistics that negative stress is rampant in our daily lives, among which are the following.

- Researchers at Yale University found that stress reduces the volume of gray matter in the areas of the brain responsible for self-control. So, experiencing stress actually makes it more difficult to deal with future stress because it diminishes your ability to take control of the situation, manage your stress, and keep things from getting out of hand—a vicious cycle if there ever was one.[3] Sadly, Ken was a perfect example of this situation.

- As research on decision-making shows, our brains are wired to be more reactionary under stress. This can mean that stressed-out leaders resort to making all-or-nothing choices, limiting the more creative possibilities available to them. In tough moments, we reach for premature and oversimplified black-and-white conclusions rather than opening ourselves to more and potentially better options.[4]

- Numerous studies show that job stress is by far the major source of stress for American adults and that it has escalated progressively over the past few decades. Increased levels of job stress, as defined by the perception of having little control but lots of demands, have been linked with increased rates of heart attack, hypertension, and other disorders.[5]

- Workplace stress is costing employers $500 billion annually because 38 percent of U.S. employees who miss work due to on-the-job stress may be absent from work for six days or more per month.[6] And as work piles up, more stress is waiting for them upon their return.

- Stress-related health problems could be responsible for between 5 to 8 percent of annual healthcare costs in the U.S. That amounts to about $180 billion each year in healthcare expenses[7] that will be passed on to workers with health benefits through rising premiums.

Stress Manifests Itself Mentally and Physically

Prolonged negative stress left unchecked can lead to one or more of the following mental and physical health issues.[8]

Mental
- Cognitive impairment. This impact forces us to become reactive to situations rather than proactive.

- Mood swings. Our uncontrolled emotions such as anger, sadness, and guilt serve as precursors to depression.

- Anxiety disorders and frequent panic attacks. These leave us exhausted.

- Prescription drug and alcohol addiction. We use chemicals to numb our stress instead of dealing with it. This is especially concerning given that prescription drug abuse is a serious and growing problem in the United States.

Physical

- Heart disease and stroke. The stress hormone cortisol (the "bad" stress hormone) makes our blood pressure and cholesterol levels rise, and to deal with our stress, we may choose unhealthy habits that affect our hearts such as smoking, physical inactivity, and overeating.

- Rapid aging. Stress takes a toll on your face in the form of dark circles, wrinkles, eye bags, hair loss, and acne.[9]

- Impaired immune system. Stress decreases the body's lymphocytes—the white blood cells that help fight off infection. The lower your lymphocyte level, the more at risk you are of catching viruses, including the common cold and cold sores.[10]

- Digestive disorders. Stress can cause a range of gastrointestinal problems, including cramping, bloating, inflammation, and a loss of appetite.[11]

- Increased body pain. Headaches, back pain, and shoulder and neck stiffness are all common with increased stress.

- Weight gain and diabetes. As I learned the hard way, stress releases cortisol and puts a lot of pressure on our bodies. Cortisol levels rise during tension-filled times. This can turn our overeating into a habit, which results in weight gain around our midsection—the unhealthiest type of fat. Because increased levels of this hormone also help cause higher insulin levels, our blood sugar drops and we crave sugary, fatty foods. So, instead of a salad or a banana, we're more likely to reach for cookies or mac and cheese. That's why they're called "comfort foods." Over time, this increased stress on our bodies may cause our pancreas to fail, meaning that we can't produce enough insulin to regulate blood sugars and we become diabetic. When we become diabetic, that opens the door for a whole host of new physical complications and expense for proper treatment.

More stress = more cortisol = higher appetite for junk food = more belly fat[12]

With the stresses associated with longer workweeks and our "always on" technology-driven lives, there is no surprise the United States has an obesity crisis on its hands, according to the Centers for Disease Control and Prevention (CDC).

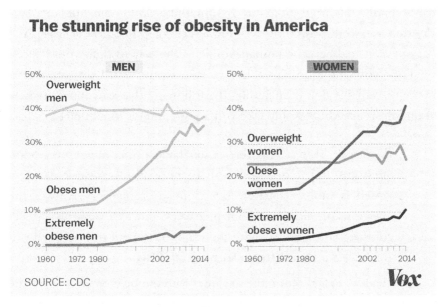

Image courtesy of Vox.com[13]

You see, from a physical standpoint, your system was designed back in the Stone Age to deal with stress. The "fight or flight" syndrome worked wonders when you had to outrun a saber-toothed tiger. But today's "always on" society equates more to mental stress. If you perceive that a situation will threaten your career or reputation, for example, it will be perceived as dangerous and elicit mental stress.[14] In other words, your perception is your reality.

And when you continually let mental stress churn in your mind, your emotional reaction may result in a release of cortisol that, in turn, suppresses your immune system, leaving you more susceptible to a range of illnesses. And if you are already dealing with physical or mental illnesses, stress can also exacerbate your symptoms and hinder your recovery efforts.[15]

Yikes.

Measuring Your Current Stress

If you are familiar with the 12-step recovery program, you would know that step one of most programs is something along the lines of: "We admitted we were powerless over the effects of [*insert item or issue*], and that our lives had become unmanageable." One way to figure out if stress is making your life unmanageable is to take a stress test. There are several free ones available online, including the following that asks approximately 40 questions and should only take you a few minutes to complete:

- *Psychologist World*. This one is my favorite because it asks good questions and it only asks you to rate your last week of stress, which is more accurately stored in your memory. Answer the questions in relation to your past week and *Psychologist World* will compare your answers with the scale to find out how stressed you are. Access it here: **http://snip.ly/a9y0hw**

- Healthy Place. This quiz asks questions about your stress over the last 12 months. Access it here: **https://www.healthyplace.com/psychological-tests/online-stress-test/**

- Holmes and Rahe. This also focuses on stressful situations you have experienced over the last 12 months. Access it here: **http://snip.ly/ogyxpi**

- Edmund Bourne. This is a simple checklist from Bourne's *The Anxiety and Phobia Workbook*. Access it here: http://snip.ly/vqcte1

You will notice that each scale asks you some of the same questions, so you might want to complete more than one of them and compare results. If one or more of the tests indicate that you are indeed stressed, I have good news for you! You are on the road to recovery. You have picked up this book and admitted that the effects of stress have become unmanageable and that you need some tools to help you cope better.

Let me return to Ken, my friend I mentioned at the beginning of the chapter. He, unfortunately, never took a stress quiz that could have provided insight into what he was doing to himself. Instead, he ended up in the ER. His intestines were inflamed with cancer, and he needed to have more than two-thirds of his intestines removed. After surgery, he had to undergo several rounds of chemotherapy.

During this time, we would talk once every 4 to 5 weeks (in between chemotherapy treatments) either on the phone or in person. He told me on several occasions that he was convinced stress caused his cancer. Whether that was true or not, he and I certainly believed it. In 2014, approximately two years after his initial surgery, and only a few weeks after his last round of chemotherapy, Ken passed away at the age of 48. That is way too early to die, and in Ken's case it might have been avoidable if only he had handled his stress better. Instead of taking action through stress coaching, tools and/ or therapy, he kept internalizing his stress until it got the best of him. Don't let it get the better of you.

Ken and me a few months before he got sick.

In the next chapter you will learn about the seven elements of the LIGHTEN™ Model that need to be aligned for your stress relief efforts to be successful long term. And then in the following chapters we'll get right into the tools that you can use immediately, several of which were inspired by my dear friend Ken's story.

Remember that stress doesn't come from what's going on in your life. It comes from your thoughts about what's going on in your life.

—ANDREW BERNSTEIN, AMERICAN PHILOSOPHER

CHAPTER 2

Seven Keys to Stress-Relief Success Using the LIGHTEN™ Model

Set peace of mind as your highest goal and organize your life around it.

—BRIAN TRACY, CANADIAN MOTIVATIONAL
SPEAKER AND AUTHOR

One of my first clients referred me to his boss who was dealing with a lot of personal issues that were causing him stress. I scheduled a time to call him, and the first thing he asked was, "So, what do you do?" I responded with my elevator pitch: "I inspire working professionals with stress relief tools that help them overcome their barriers and obstacles to success."

"Interesting," my friend's boss says. "I've tried a few techniques myself, but I haven't been able to make them stick." And that was an *aha-moment* for me. I had been working with several clients already, and many of them didn't have the foundation necessary to maintain success after they had worked with me. My bad. I was so eager to help these clients right away that I jumped into application work before fully assessing and educating them on the importance of their foundation for success. Using business terminology, I was providing stress relief tools (tactics) without a foundation of balance that each of my clients should strive for (strategy).

The foundational basis or groundwork for effective and holistic long-term stress relief success is what I call the LIGHTEN™ Model. I am a visual person, so I demonstrate the model in a simple diagram that was inspired by a Southwest Airlines flight attendant who once described the button passengers should push for additional lighting as a "hairy light bulb." The humor of this description is appropriate because it is a bright reminder to not take ourselves so seriously that we stress about it.

The LIGHTEN™ Model diagram represents the idea (hence the light bulb) that there are seven areas that need to be nurtured and in alignment to maximize stress-relief efforts, which we will explore one by one.

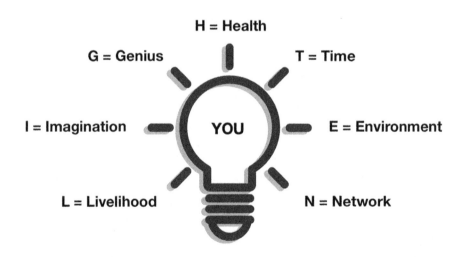

LIGHTEN™ Model For Stress Relief

L: Livelihood (career)

The average American spends 90,000 hours at work over their lifetime.[16] Think about that. We are likely to spend more time at work than we spend with our loved ones, and many of us with workaholic tendencies will work more hours than we sleep. Technology often exacerbates this situation, as it allows us to check messages on our phones at all hours of the day, so we never have true downtime.

In the business of sales, you have the stress of hitting your quota, and even if you have been a top performer in the past, the "what have you done for me lately?" response from your sales manager is always looming. Why? Because in sales it's all about the revenue you generate in the current month, quarter or year.

If you are in marketing, you don't have the short-term deliverable that sales does, but you are closely aligned to their revenue goals. If the sales team doesn't hit its numbers, inevitably senior management looks for cost-cutting options and the marketing budget and staff can be prime targets. If you are fortunate enough to be working at a company that is hitting its numbers, you still have the pressures of delivering high-quality work on time and on budget. As marketers, everyone else in the organization critiques your work, be it a website, brochure, ad, you name it—so you are constantly under scrutiny for the work you do.

If your career is sucking your energy, or even if it just seems that way, getting some balance will be extremely important. There are a lot of stress relief tools you can try quickly and easily to get you moving in the right direction. Start with the chapter for "**L**" in the LIGHTEN™ Model.

I: Imagination (active mind)

If you are not old enough to remember the "Calgon take me away" commercials from the 1970s and 1980s, find it on YouTube.[17] This ad shows you what imagination can do to help you get out of a stressful situation. Maybe you imagine hitting your quota and getting a sales award, rather than imagining missing your goal. Maybe you imagine giving a great presentation capped with a standing ovation, rather than succumbing to your fear of public speaking. Whatever the challenge that lies ahead for you, your imagination can help you overcome it.

In the "I" chapter of this book, the stress relief tools will require you to imagine something, so you will need to let the creative side of your brain have a little fun as you visualize overcoming your stressful situation. Your active mind—which makes up 5 percent of your brain activity—allows you to focus on visualizing something that is totally new and unique; something you've never physically experienced before.[18]

G: Genius (unconscious mind)

As mentioned in the previous chapter, most stress is mental. We tend to let things fester in our mind, and if we focus on negative outcomes, we put unnecessary stress on ourselves. When we fixate on the trouble we have sleeping, or maintaining our diet, we can become exhausted.

It's imperative that you find stress relief tools that work for you to calm your mind. And while the imagination part of your active mind is important, equally important will be your ability to get in touch with your unconscious mind. Your unconscious mind is your autopilot. It runs your body 24 hours a day, seven days a week. It is also in charge of things like:

- Memory. The unconscious mind stores the everyday things such as your telephone number, how to drive a car, what you need to get from the shop on the way home, and so on.

- Daily behaviors and habits.

- Filters, such as beliefs and values. You unconsciously run information through your brain to test their validity according to your perception of the world, things like politics and religion.

- Sensations. Your unconcious mind will assess information taken in via your five senses according to what it means to you (your likes and dislikes).

I have had significant training in neurolinguistic programming (NLP), which describes the fundamental dynamics between the mind (neuro) and language (linguistic) and how their interplay affects our body and behavior (programming). With NLP, long-term stress relief happens on the unconscious level, so you have to make sure your unconscious and active minds are in alignment.

Please refer to the "**G**" chapter for stress relief tools aligned to this topic, including Parts Integration, as well as Mental and Emotional Release (MER), that specifically come from NLP.

H: Health

I believe "**H**" is the most important part of the LIGHTEN™ Model, hands down. Health is the inspiration for writing this book. If you don't have your health, nothing else really matters. You won't have the energy or the willingness to take action.

Let's say you have a leg injury—how easy is it to make a sales call? If you have a migraine, do the marketing ideas come rolling out? When you have had a bad flu, do you want to do anything other than sleep? Me neither.

Taking care of the body you have is essential, and the "**H**" chapter will give you the tools to do this quickly and easily.

T: Time

Like health, this one is easy to comprehend. Do you have to hit your quota by a certain date? Yes. Does an important project on your plate have to be completed by a certain date? Yes. So, is timing related to stress? Yes.

Time is also important because you have a limited amount of it, and once it's gone, you can never get it back. You need to treat it like an asset and take action, such as trying a few tools and techniques in this book TODAY, not tomorrow or next week. Act right now. Why? Because humans by nature don't like change and, indeed, experimenting with a new stress-relief tool is change.

Commit to taking action and trying different tools included in the "**T**" chapter until you have a handful of go-to techniques that can help you save your precious time.

E: Environment

Your environment—whether it is at work, school or home—is critical to your success. If you are trying to make a sales call and there is noise all around you, you will be distracted. If you are trying to concentrate on finishing your budget and there are constant interruptions, you will be sidetracked. If your desk chair or other furniture is not comfortable or ergonomic, you will be too uncomfortable to concentrate.

When you get distracted, you don't accomplish anything other than delaying what you are trying to complete. And when you get delayed, what typically comes next? Yep, you guessed it: additional stress.

Some stress-relief tools need silence to implement effectively. Some techniques will need you to sit down awhile. Whatever tool(s) you decide to implement from the "**E**" chapter of this book, make sure the environment around you is supportive of your efforts.

N: Network (relationships)

The people in your life matter. Your family, friends and significant other play a huge role in your stress level, directly affecting your interactions with those personal relationships.

Stress depletes us, sapping our cognitive resources. It also increases vigilance. This means when you are stressed, you are more likely to notice negative behaviors and less able to stop yourself from reacting badly to them. It also means that you are less patient with the people around you and less able to give them the benefit of the doubt when they behave badly.

Stress also makes people more irritable and hostile, which increases the likelihood of fighting. And during a disagreement, stress makes people less able to listen properly or show interest and empathy. In short, stress turns non-issues into issues and impairs your ability to deal with it constructively.[19]

The stresses in your personal and professional relationships can cross over into other areas of your life. For example, an unsupportive supervisor will add anxiety to your workday that you then take home to your family. Or a fight with a loved one at home may raise your blood pressure or glucose levels, potentially affecting your health and your career.

If relationships in your life are particularly challenging for you, check out the "**N**" chapter for some tools that can help you.

The Reality of the LIGHTEN™ Model

Okay, I bet I know what you are thinking: if you had every aspect of the LIGHTEN™ Model in alignment you wouldn't need stress relief. And you are right! Think of the LIGHTEN™ Model as your utopia that you aspire to achieve. Each part of the model needs care and nurturing. However, sometimes you will need to focus more attention on only one or two areas of the model. That's okay because the model is flexible and designed to work within your parameters and current pressures.

The model's intent is to serve as a reminder that each area plays an important role in your stress-relief efforts. Sometimes work will take a toll on your relationships, especially when there are looming deadlines; your mind—both active and unconscious—start racing. You forget to clean up after yourself, and your environment becomes cluttered and difficult to work or live in. The constant worry eventually affects your health through a lack of sleep, poor diet, and limited exercise. You end up lacking the energy to take care of what was bothering you in the first place, which compounds your stress. See how it all interrelates? That's the power of the LIGHTEN™ Model—a bright idea in the form of a hairy light bulb that has come to you in a playful and useful way.

And because every aspect of the LIGHTEN™ Model interrelates, so do most of the stress relief tips, tools, and techniques included in the following chapters. Therefore, each suggestion will have a key with the letter(s) highlighted in the word LIGHTEN™ to let you know that this tip, tool or technique applies to that particular topic or topics of the model. For example:

L I G H T E N ™ = *the suggestion can help with your Livelihood, Health, and Network*

 = *indicates tool that author uses personally for his stress relief*

 = *shortcut to implementing tool without reading the introductory text*

Just think how fun it will be to explain to your friends, family, and coworkers how a bright and hairy light bulb helped you reduce stress!

I cannot conclude this chapter without thanking my friend's boss for reminding me that you have to have a foundation (strategy) in place before you start implementing tools (tactics). Once I developed the model, I went back to him, and he liked it enough to start working with me to address relationship issues (**N**etwork) that were affecting his focus at work (**L**ivelihood). After successfully completing some stress relief activities, he referred me to a colleague of his, all because of this new foundational structure.

Many of us feel stress and get overwhelmed not because we're taking on too much, but because we're taking on too little of what really strengthens us.

—MARCUS BUCKINGHAM, BRITISH AUTHOR

CHAPTER 3

LIVELIHOOD–
Tips, Tools, and Techniques
for a More Enjoyable Workday
and Career

I am not a product of my circumstances.
I am a product of my decisions.

—STEPHEN COVEY, AMERICAN EDUCATOR AND AUTHOR

One of the most common questions we are asked is "What do you do?" Whether you have a good elevator speech to answer the question, the fact remains that our identity is closely tied with our livelihood. Throughout my career I've had the honor of holding many titles, such as salesperson, marketing director, professor, and small-business owner. While each of my career roles has come with its fair share of challenges, being a small-business owner was probably the most stressful for me. I knew that if I failed, several dominoes would fall as well: employees would lose their jobs, I would lose my investment of time and money in the business, and my family would see me as a failure (that last one was just my perception, not based on fact). The stress I manifested certainly contributed to the perfect storm that resulted in diabetes. And it also had an impact on my decision to go back to the corporate world. I traded the pressure of running my own business to that of an employee, exchanging one type of stress for another. That was an interesting lesson I will discuss later in this chapter.

As you reflect on your career thus far, which titles and experiences are you most proud of? Those are the ones that reflect your professional identity. And in order to nurture your professional identity, you need to effectively handle the inevitable pressure that comes your way. Give one or more of the following stress-relief suggestions a try and see how your overall outlook to your profession improves.

Remember: *Each suggestion will have a key with the letter(s) highlighted in the word LIGHTEN™ to let you know that this tip, tool, or technique applies to that particular topic or topics of the model.*

 = Author Uses Personally

 = Shortcut to Implementation

Gratitude

(LIGHTEN™: Livelihood, Imagination, Health, Environment, and Network)

Gratitude for someone or something you already have has the ability to attract what you want in life. It will improve your relationships and your health, reduce negativity, and help you learn. Thousands of articles have been written about the power of gratitude, and I can attest firsthand that it has helped me immensely.

I make it a nightly habit that right before I go to sleep, I ask my wife what she is grateful for, and she does the same for me. I typically start with my health, and then recap other things that happened during the day that I am grateful for. I'm specific about what I am thankful for because that trains my mind to think in a more grateful way. For example, I might say "I'm grateful for my health because it allowed me to participate in a hike today; thank you, thank you, thank you." I learned to say thank you three times from a favorite book of mine.[20]

I also use gratitude for simple stuff, such as making it through a green light, having a meal I like, hot water in the shower, and so on. We take a lot for granted, and if we start appreciating the little things more, we prepare ourselves for the more difficult challenges, challenges like not wanting to be at work.

If not wanting to go to work resonates with you, try writing down what you are grateful for about your job and why. These might include the things your paycheck pays for (like bills), the healthcare and retirement benefits your employer provides, or the coworkers you enjoy talking with. If you give gratitude as the first thing you do at work, you will be amazed at how much better the beginning of your workday will start. And if the beginning of your day starts well, who's to say you can't keep that positive momentum up for the rest of the day? Before you know it, you are heading home with more energy after a less stressful day.

> ### Lighten your day (1 minute):
>
> *Write down FIVE things about your job you are grateful for when you first get to your desk. Think about what your paycheck enables you to do, the health benefits you receive to keep you and your family healthy, the friendships with coworkers you have established, etc.*
>
> *By doing this at the beginning of your workday, you set yourself up for a less stressful day. Repeat this daily for ONE WEEK and notice the impact on your overall mood.*

Don't Multitask

(**LIGH**TEN™: **L**ivelihood, **I**magination, **G**enius, and **T**ime)

Do a simple search on Google about multitasking and hundreds of articles will come up promoting its perils.

Unfortunately, our brains just aren't equipped for multitasking work. When you're trying to accomplish two dissimilar tasks, each one requiring some level of consideration and attention, multitasking falls apart. Your brain just can't take in and process two simultaneous, separate streams of information and encode them fully into short-term memory. And when information doesn't make it into short-term memory, it can't be transferred into long-term memory for recall later.[21]

In fact, the true cost of multitasking can be enormous on the actual time we spend on each project. Each time we switch context, i.e., move from one project to the next, it costs us valuable time as we mentally engage to the level that we're ready to work on that new assignment. Researchers found that when we are only concentrating on one project during an eight-hour day, we can focus 100 percent of our time to that task.

When we have two projects, we lose 20 percent of our time recalibrating between projects (figuring out where we left off, re-reading the work, etc.). As the number of projects we are working on during the day goes up, the calibration time goes up too. If we have five projects during the day, calibration takes up 80 percent of our time. This means that we are only able to provide 4 percent of our time during the day to each of those five undertakings (i.e., 20 percent of project time divided by five), making the completion of those projects much slower.[22]

Bottom line: multitasking works against you. It's making you less efficient, not more. And when you are less efficient, the work piles up. And when the work piles up, your stress level increases. Do yourself and your career, peers, family, and friends a favor and be fully present for each of your responsibilities. Do not split between multiple projects because your brain doesn't work proportionately to your priorities.

 "I'm a busy marketing communications professional. I felt like I had to multitask just to keep up. However, I now realize I was getting less done and the work that was getting done often had errors. I stopped multitasking, and I now feel like I get more done by not constantly switching back and forth."

—MARIA M., CLIENT

Lighten your day (1 minute):

When you are in a meeting, close your laptop, turn your phone off, and have a pen and notepad. Resist the temptation to check your email or texts. Take notes on paper if necessary. Ask others in your meeting to follow suit so that everyone is engaged and focused on the meeting agenda. After the meeting, ask for clarity on what the next steps are, minimizing stressful miscommunication.

End-of-Day Anchor

(**LI**GHTEN™: **L**ivelihood, **I**magination, **T**ime, and **E**nvironment)

When I was young in my career, I did sales for FedEx. I was always amazed at how our couriers who delivered and picked up the packages looked 10 to 20 years younger than they actually were. I assumed it was the exercise they got as part of their job, yet several of them told me that it was because they could mentally clock out at the end of the day.

Many of us have a difficult time turning off our work mode at the end of the day, and so we bring work home. If this sounds like you, consider developing an end-of-day anchor routine that, with habit, will signal to your brain that your workday has indeed ended. Signals might include locking your office door, turning off your monitor, or calling home. Consistent use of this designated anchor will enable you to take control of your emotions and shift your mental state, just as if you were clocking out on a timesheet.[23]

My end-of-day anchor is when I hear the garage door open. That signals to me that my wife is home and I need to be present for her. I greet her at the door and then wrap up whatever I was working on, saving it for the next day.

👍 "Stress can definitely add years to someone's life, and having the self-awareness to start an end–of–day plan has been very important for me."

—TERESA H., CLIENT

Lighten your day (1 minute):

Think of something that you would only do once at the end of your workday and make that a habit to signal to your brain that your work is done. Maybe it is washing out your water glass or coffee cup. It could be turning off your computer or calling home to let your loved ones know you are on your way. Whatever it is, put a reminder in your phone at the same time every day until it becomes a habit.

Email Purge

(**LI**GHTE**N**™: **L**ivelihood, and **N**etwork)

One of my former coworkers taught me this. If you get a ton of email at work (who doesn't?), rather than going through the deluge of hundreds or thousands of messages after returning from a one-week vacation, consider just deleting everything WITHOUT looking at it. If it is really important, then the sender will follow up with you. In most cases, the situation will have already rectified itself or it wasn't important enough for you to attend to upon your return.

This also applies if you haven't been on vacation, but you have been too busy to get to all your email for weeks or months. This will give you the freedom to start fresh and eliminate the stress associated with feeling overwhelmed with all those old emails.

Of course, you must use commonsense when using this technique. If you are obligated to respond to emails from customers, management, or regulatory officials, for example, you want to be mindful about which emails to mass eliminate with your delete key.

 "I was three weeks out of the office. I came back to several hundred emails, and I had no idea where to start. I decided to filter my email, and I purged anything that didn't come from my boss. I was worried I was going to get fired, but nothing happened other than I got out from my email overload. What a relief!"

—Veronica G., client

Lighten your day (1 minute):

When your unread email is more than 100 and you are worried about where you will find the time to read each message, do the following for instant stress relief:

1. *Click on the first unread message.*

2. *Hold the shift key down and click on the last unread message.*

3. *Press the delete key.*

4. *Take one deep breath and get on with your day.*

Prioritize Tasks

(**L**IGHTEN™: **L**ivelihood, **I**magination, **H**ealth, **T**ime, and **N**etwork)

If you are an overachiever like me, prioritizing your tasks is a must for stress management. I have a simple process I have used for years that I am going to share, as well as another slightly more methodical process that has been successfully used for over 100 years.

To decide how much time to spend on tasks, I write down everything I have on my plate. Then I draw two columns and rate each item by their importance (high, medium, low) to my career, relationships, health, and so on and urgency (also high, medium, low). Those that are "high" in both categories are given priority; those that are classified high in one category and medium in the other get second priority; and those that have two mediums get third priority of my time. Anything with a low rating in either category can wait. At the end of the day, I reprioritize based on what still needs to be done.

The slightly more methodical way is called the Ivy Lee Method:

1) At the end of each workday, write down the six most important things you need to accomplish tomorrow. Do not write down more than six tasks.

2) Prioritize those six items in order of their true importance.

3) When you arrive tomorrow, concentrate only on the first task. Work until the first task is finished before moving on to the second task.

4) Approach the rest of your list in the same fashion. At the end of the day, move any unfinished items to a new list of six tasks for the following day.[24]

5) Repeat this process every working day.

The reason I use my method is because sometimes the situation dictates that I cannot focus only on one project before working on another project. Therefore, my method allows for a little more flexibility as my day goes on. However, if you choose to follow my process, that does not mean you should multitask. Whichever method you use, the final act of reprioritizing at the end of the day gives you a sense of completion and stress relief.

Lighten your day (5 minutes):

To be more impactful at work and minimize your stress level, do the following:

1. *Write down everything you have on your plate.*

2. *Draw two columns and rate each item by their importance (high, medium, low) and urgency (also high, medium, low).*

3. *Place those that are rated high on both scales as first priority of your time, those that have one high and one medium get second priority of your time, and those that have two mediums get third priority of your time. Anything with a low rating can wait.*

4. *At the end of the day, reprioritize based on what still needs to be done.*

Take Microbreaks
(**LI**GHTEN™: **L**ivelihood, **I**magination, and **N**etwork)

Do you find yourself continuing to work even though you are tired or overwhelmed? If this is commonplace, you need to understand that this decreases your productivity and increases the chance that you will make mistakes. Instead of pushing yourself beyond what is healthy, take a microbreak. You will feel refreshed and ready to take on so much more when you return.

A microbreak is timeout that you should take whenever you need it. It should be unscheduled and informal. It should also be taken in between work tasks, not in the middle of a task, to avoid interrupting workflow and concentration. A microbreak could last anywhere from a few seconds to several minutes, and it should involve healthy and relaxing activities, such as going for a quick walk, completing a puzzle game or having a friendly chat with a colleague. Anything work related is a no-no.[25]

👍 *"Yesterday, I took the first of many microbreaks. Because I took the break in between my projects, I was able to come back refreshed and focused on the next task. It's an excellent concept!"*

—SCOTT M., CLIENT

Lighten your day (10 minutes):

When you are in between projects (when one is completed or waiting on someone else's desk for review) take a microbreak for 10 minutes to refresh your mind and body while also decompressing your stress level. It can be a quick walk, stretching, a friendly conversation with a coworker or friend/ family member. Just don't think or talk about work for the microbreak to work its magic.

Weekly Reflection

(**LI**GHTEN™: **L**ivelihood and **I**magination)

Weekly reflection is a powerful tool for improvement. While I am not a big fan of doing work on the weekend, I understand the realities of today's working professionals. Spending a few minutes of your time off considering work scenarios can pay great dividends later.

Use the weekend to contemplate the larger forces that are shaping your industry, your organization, and your job. Without the distractions of Monday to Friday busy work, you should be able to see things in a whole new light. Use this insight to alter your approach to the coming week, improving the efficiency and efficacy of your work.[26] And similarly to the "Plan Your Day" technique, this process gives you a sense of control and thus decreases your stress level.

Lighten your day (15-30 minutes):

Each weekend, block out 15 to 30 minutes when you can have some quiet time to reflect on your week ahead. Are there any insights you have that can help improve your performance and/or reduce potential stress? If so, note them down and review them again before you arrive at work on Monday.

Detox from Technology

(**LI**GHTEN™: **L**ivelihood, **I**magination, **H**ealth, **T**ime, **E**nvironment, and **N**etwork)

Disconnecting from your electronic communication leash (also known as your work cell phone) is very important. If you can't find a way to remove yourself electronically from your work, then you've never really left the office.

Making yourself available 24/7 exposes you to a constant barrage of stressors that prevent you from refocusing and recharging. And research shows that people who merely feel they have to answer work emails during non-work hours were more anxious and reported more relationship stress and poorer health.[27]

If taking the entire weekend off handling work emails and calls isn't realistic, try designating specific times on Saturday and Sunday for checking emails and responding to voicemails. For example, check your messages on Saturday afternoon while your kids are getting a haircut and/or on Sunday evenings after dinner. Scheduling short blocks of time will alleviate stress without sacrificing availability.[28]

And if you can spare a few days away from the office, a great way to detox from your phone is to go camping in a location that has no cell service or WiFi. When I camp, I usually go through an electronics detox that first day. On the second day, I realize that the world hasn't ended, and I can be fully present with my friends and family.

 "I used to check my emails during family outings and not being present. Now I intentionally leave my phone in the car. That way I stay in the present and enjoy important moments."

—GARY L., CLIENT

Lighten your day (1 hour):

This weekend, power your phone off for one hour. Notice that the world didn't stop spinning for that time? Expand your phone-free time each weekend and/or evening until you have found a healthy balance.

Realize You Can't Do It All

(**LIGHTEN**™: **L**ivelihood, **T**ime, and **N**etwork)

I grew up a perfectionist because I was always striving for my father's approval. No matter what I excelled at as a child, my father always found something to nitpick. Fortunately, as an adult I got over that using various self-help techniques, and I even had the wonderful opportunity to make amends with my father when he was in hospice. I discovered during his last days that he was truly proud of me, and that helped me reduce my obsession to do everything impeccably.

Not being a perfectionist means accepting that you can't do everything. As author Jon Acuff says: "You only have two options right now: 1. Attempt more than is humanly possible and fail. 2. Choose what to bomb and succeed at a goal that matters."[29]

Bombs away!

> *Lighten your day (1 hour):*
>
> *When you have a long task list, concentrate only on those items you know you can do well. Delegate the ones you cannot possibly get to and/or complete satisfactorily and be okay with not being a perfectionist.*

Communicate Workplace Stresses to Your Employer

(**LIGHTEN**™: **L**ivelihood, **E**nvironment, and **N**etwork)

You spend approximately one-third of your life (not including evenings and weekends) at work when you are employed full-time. And it is expected that you will experience some level of stress on a regular basis.

However, if you feel like workplace stresses are consistently affecting your performance, consider speaking with your employer, either your supervisor or the human resources department.

Healthy and happy employees are more productive, and it is difficult to replace productive and dependable employees. Therefore, your employer has an incentive to tackle workplace stress whenever possible.

Make sure that what you communicate is constructive and actionable for your employer. Rather than rattle off a list of complaints, let your employer know about specific conditions that are impacting your work performance, along with a few ideas on what you think could be done to improve the situation.[30]

Lighten your day (1 hour):

When something at work beyond your control is stressing you out, be proactive and speak to your supervisor or human resources department. Communicate specific conditions that are impacting your work performance (not complaints), along with a few ideas on what you think could be done to improve the situation. It is in your employer's best interest to keep good employees, and the simple act of communicating what is not working for you will provide much needed stress relief.

Overcome Imposter Syndrome
(**L**IGHTEN™: **L**ivelihood and **N**etwork)

Have you ever had that feeling that you are not qualified for the role you currently hold? Most if not all of us have. It's basically a limiting belief generated by your inner critic who's hell bent on creating unnecessary stress in your professional life (refer to the "Talk to Yourself" suggestion for more information). There are two approaches you can take to overcome imposter syndrome.

The first approach is to write down the reasons you think you're an imposter. By writing them down, you are allowing them to be expressed more fully, which dissipates some of their power. The key thing to keep in mind is you are not agreeing that any of these thoughts are true, rational, or even proper English! Next, concentrate on why you might feel and think these things, whether they are true or not. Write those down along with any themes or patterns you notice. By having awareness of your beliefs and patterns, you can then plan a better approach. Write the new approach down and put it into action.[31]

If the first approach doesn't work for you, the second approach would be working with a professional trained in Mental and Emotional Release (MER) that is discussed later in this book. MER allows you to dig down and remove limiting beliefs you have that have been festering and creating stress for many years.

👍 "I was recently promoted and felt like I was going to disappoint my boss. By doing a MER (Mental and Emotional Release) session with Professor Alexander, I realized that my fear was rooted in my childhood experiences with my father. After the release work we did, I now feel confident and successful at my job."

—Steven B., client

Lighten your day (1 hour):

If you feel like you are over your head and don't qualify for your current position, do the following:

1. *Write down reasons you think you're not qualified.*

2. *Concentrate on why you might feel and think these things, whether they are true or not. Write those down along with any themes or patterns you notice.*

3. *Review your notes, and then plan a new approach. Write the new approach down and put it into action.*

4. *If steps 1-3 are not successful, work with a professional trained in Mental and Emotional Release (MER) to remove your limiting beliefs.*

Decide to Stay or Quit Your Job

(**LIGHTEN**™: **L**ivelihood, **I**magination, **G**enius, **H**ealth, **E**nvironment, and **N**etwork)

Leaving your job is one of the most stressful decisions you may have to make. For some of us, this is a dilemma that has come up many times throughout our career. If you have a bad boss or an opportunity that offers more pay and a bunch of other great benefits, the decision is easy. But what if that decision isn't so black and white? Churning over that decision can create anxiety.

Many years ago, I coauthored a book titled *Money Isn't All That Matters: Strategies for Attracting and Retaining Technical Professionals*. One of the key findings in the book was that employees don't leave companies as much as they leave their managers. The relationship with their manager was the true determining factor in whether an employee stayed at the organization.[32]

How do you feel about your manager? If your boss fired you right now, what would your reaction be? If you think you would be relieved, you should quit. If you believe you would be devastated, that suggests you don't really want to quit.[33] It's a simple decision. Of course, if you ultimately decide not to quit, think about why you considered quitting in the first place and come up with a strategy to address that issue so that you can be more satisfied at work.

Another way you can assess your situation is with a pros/cons list. You can organize it based on your interests (refer to "Determine Your Personal Values" technique for more information) and then rank your current job and a potential new job based on how well they align with what is important to you. For this technique to work, make sure you are honest with your rankings.

If you are more of a visual person, you could use a flowchart to help you decide. The one from The Job Network[34] is a little whimsical, but I like how it gets you to think of a few factors and steps you should take to make the right decision.

Whatever you decide, understand that it is in your best interest to make a final decision. The longer you let the decision fester, the more stress you will have.

👍 "I felt miserable and unappreciated at my job, constantly micromanaged by my boss. I wanted to leave but felt responsible for my family. By asking myself what my reaction would be if my boss fired me today, I actually felt relieved and free. I decided to leave that job, and now I am making six figures at my own company."

—AARON S., CLIENT

Lighten your day (1 hour):

If you are contemplating whether to stay or quit your job, ask yourself this question: If your boss fired you right now, what would your reaction be? If you would be relieved, you should quit. If you would be devastated, obviously that means you don't want to quit. If you don't want to quit, figure out what got you to ask that question in the first place and take steps to address that with your current position so that you can be more satisfied at work.

Map Your "Ikigai"

(**LIGHTEN**™: **L**ivelihood, **I**magination, **H**ealth, and **T**ime)

Pronounced ee-kee-guy, *Iikigai* is most often translated as "a reason for being." The premise is when you bring together what you love, what you are good at, what the world needs, and what you can be paid for, that is when you have found your ikigai.[35] Once you have found your reason for life, your health will improve

A Venn diagram on the next page, shows *ikigai* situated at the center point of what you love, what you are good at, what the world needs, and what you can make income from. Finding the answers to these four questions and figuring out how they all work in alignment will provide you with a sense of peacefulness and purpose.

Image courtesy of the Yoga Hub[36]

A similar visual approach is a Transformational Mandala, where you draw a circle in the middle that represents you or your spirit. Then you draw additional elements around your center circle that represent the important areas of your life (such as love, health, wealth, and personal self-expression) as it relates to your inner spirit, with the goal of keeping all these key areas in balance. The LIGHTEN™ Model diagram is a form of Transformational Mandala because it shows the parts of your life you need to balance to sustain long-lasting stress relief.

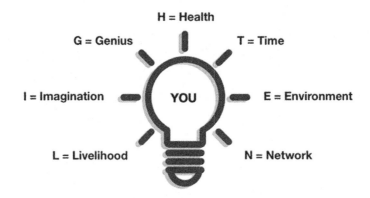

LIGHTEN™ Model For Stress Relief

What's fun about both the ikigai and Transformational Mandala is that you can update and modify the areas of your life that are important and keep a visual representation as a reminder to maintain balance.

Lighten your day (1 hour):

1. *In four separate lists, write down what you love to do, what you are good at, what the world needs, and what you can make money from.*

2. *Review each list and come up with a one- or two-word title for each list.*

3. *Refer to the Venn diagram above, and draw four intersecting circles and place the list titles into the four circles (one per circle).*

4. *Study your diagram and ask your unconscious mind to help you come up with your ikigai. Note that you might have to sleep on it or ponder this for several days to come up with the best answer.*

5. *Take a picture of this drawing with your smartphone and also place this image somewhere visible (your desk, your dresser, your car) to serve as a reminder that what is important to you should remain in balance.*

Write a Personal Mission Statement

(**LIGHTEN**™: **L**ivelihood, **I**magination, **H**ealth, **E**nvironment, and **N**etwork)

Mission statements are not just for companies: they work for individuals as well. Writing a personal mission statement offers the opportunity to establish what's important to you and can help guide you toward a decision about a particular job, company, or career field. It also enables you to chart a new course when you're at a career crossroads.[37] Some of the suggestions included in this book can help you with this process.

Creating a personal mission statement requires you to reflect upon your past successes, your core values, how you want to make a difference, and your goals. When you have completed it, you can always refer to it for direct feedback on whether the pressure you are experiencing supports or hinders your mission statement and is worth your time and attention.

Lighten your day (1 hour):

1. Write down a handful of successes you have had professionally over the last five years, and list what aspects of those successes brought you satisfaction. Pinpoint characteristics that each of those successes has in common.

2. Identify your core values. Refer to the "Determine Your Personal Values" tool for additional information.

3. Discover what difference you want to make in this world.

4. Categorize your goals in life. Refer to the "Vision Board" or "Binder" tool for a creative way to develop meaningful goals.

5. Craft your mission statement in two or three sentences that incorporates the answers you find during steps one through four above.

6. Refer to your mission statement whenever you are stressed about your career to ensure you are still on the right path, and adjust the statement as needed as you progress in your career.

Develop Your Passion

(**LIGHTEN**™: **L**ivelihood, **I**magination, **G**enius, **H**ealth, **T**ime, **E**nvironment, and **N**etwork)

I'm sure you have heard "find your passion" before. I've probably used that phrase hundreds of times myself. But what does "passion" mean in this context? We need to be clear on its definition before proceeding.

Passion is putting more energy into something than is required. It is more than just enthusiasm or excitement: it is ambition that is pursued with as much heart, mind, body, and soul as possible.[38]

However, finding your passion can be problematic. It's easy to get excited about something new. Yet, people often give up too quickly when they find out that what they thought was their passion is too much work. They think that if that passion aligned with their excitement then it should come easily, going against the old adage of "find your passion and you will never work a day in your life."

Recent research indicates we have two mindsets when it comes to passion. One is a "fixed theory of interests," the idea that core interests are there from birth and just waiting to be discovered. The other theory is a "growth theory," the idea that interests are something anyone can cultivate over time. People who think passions are inherent tend to pick jobs that fit them well from the outset because they prioritize enjoyment over good pay. People who think passions are developed, meanwhile, often prioritize other goals over immediate enjoyment at work, and they grow to fit their vocations better over time.[39]

The primary learning here is not to give up on something you initially get excited about. Your passions are there to be found and developed so that your livelihood can be true to your personal mission statement. Why? Because when you are not true to yourself, you cause yourself unnecessary stress. Jay Shetty says this best in his short video "Find Your Passion"[40] that I highly recommend you watch.

"I am passionate about fishing and was always dreaming about building a fishing retreat. After writing down the challenges and the financial cost, I wrote down a business plan to make it work. After three years of preparation and planning, I was able to fulfill my dream and my fishing resort became a reality."

—YURI G., CLIENT

Lighten your day (1 hour):

Think about something you were passionate about but gave up because of challenges you ran into. Do you still have an excitement about it? If so, write down the challenges that you could expect to occur, and then write down ways you could develop that passion further to help overcome those challenges. For example, if you wanted to start your own business but lacked time in your schedule, block out one hour every day to work on your business plan, designing your logo, refining your product/service offering, etc. As long as you are making progress each day, you will be cultivating and developing your passion.

Understand That Money Equals Life Energy

(**LIG**HTEN™: **L**ivelihood, **I**magination, **H**ealth, **T**ime, and **E**nvironment)

Finances are one of the biggest stressors we face in life. It is a major factor in why we worry about being stuck in a job or in a failing marriage. However, by understanding the true value of money in our lives, we can start directing our energies in more positive (and less stressful) ways.

According to the authors of the book *Your Money or Your Life*,[41] money is something you trade life energy for. Life energy is something you only have a limited supply of, but you have the opportunity to set new priorities for using it. The process requires you to clearly understand what you are exactly trading life energy for. This can be done in two ways:

1. Deducting from your gross monthly income the actual costs in time and money required to maintain your job. Compute your true hourly cost by including commuting costs/time, doing your taxes, and buying clothing or other items required to do your job. Also include at-work meals, amounts spent for decompressing and escaping work stress, and the impact of job-related illness, etc.

2. Keeping track of every cent that comes into or goes out of your life. A software tool like Quicken can help with this task, as long as you are diligent about tracking everything, especially your spending cash.

Just comparing the results of these two methods will give you insight into where your life energy is going. By understanding where you spend your time and money, and what you could change, you can gain back some of the life energy you are currently losing on a monthly basis. This insight might also open new possibilities for a different career interest because you have a better handle on your financial status.

👍 "Our credit card bills were sky rocketing, and it was very stressful. By downloading the Mint app, I was able to see how much I was overspending on my frequent trips to Starbucks."

—Valorie P., client

Lighten your day (1 month):

*Create an account with **quicken.com** or **mint.com** and TRACK EVERYTHING you earn and spend for one month. This needs to include all your cash spending, so if you don't have a receipt for a cash transaction (often the case when you are sharing a bill with a friend), write down a reminder of the expense. Once you have a complete month of tracking, compare the two sets of results. Are you spending your life energy appropriately? The numbers don't lie.*

Reflection Point

Now that we are at the end of this chapter, which stress relief tool did you like best? What was it about the tool you liked? Making notes to yourself below will help commit what you've learned to memory:

The stress-relief tool I like best:

I will use this tool specifically for:

The one that worked best for you should be bookmarked so you can easily refer to it in the future. You can also share it with your friends and family as a way of giving back to your community. There are also video-instruction stress relief tools available for you to review and share by visiting my blog at **PeteAlexander.com**.

At the beginning of this chapter I mentioned that the stress I encountered as a small-business owner was a factor in my decision to return to the corporate world as an employee. Had I known then about the "Livelihood" stress relief tools we explored in this chapter, I may have made a different decision. For example, I could have written my list of five things I was grateful about my small business first thing every day. That would have started me off on a positive note that could have been maintained on any normal day. Instead, I traded one type of stress—the stress of everyone depending on me—for another: the stress of living up to the expectations of a demanding supervisor.

Ironically, I learned the hard way that I was manifesting most of the stress that was occurring in my professional life. I was letting my imagination and active mind make my decisions without knowing all the true facts about what was really causing me to worry. That's why I wrote the next chapter. I want to help you avoid the mistakes I made and work effectively with your active mind.

Stress is an ignorant state. It believes that everything is an emergency.

—NATALIE GOLDBERG, AMERICAN AUTHOR

CHAPTER 4

IMAGINATION—
Tips, Tools, and Techniques
for Using Your Active Mind to
Envision a Stress-Free State

The greatest weapon against stress is our ability
to choose one thought over another.

—WILLIAM JAMES, AMERICAN PHILOSOPHER

A s a child, I had a vivid imagination. I would invent all sorts of games to keep myself entertained, with or without friends around. The ones I remember most fondly are:

- Playing with my Hot Wheels cars in the dirt with made up roads and cities.

- Make-believe baseball playoffs and World Series where I would throw a tennis ball up on the roof of my house and wait for it to bounce off to catch it (out) or not (base hit).

- Imaginary football playoffs and Super Bowl where I would throw two toy helmets of NFL teams into the air. How they landed determined whether one team won or the other.

I'm sure if you think about it, you too had games or toys that you brought to life with your imagination to pass the time. Yep, they were the good old days of having time to let your youthful imagination go wild.

As we get older and "shit happens," we tend to let the challenges of life cloud our imagination with worrying about what might happen, especially things we have little or no control over. And, as I learned the hard way, when you feel like you have no control over the situation, your negative imagination will start to manifest, causing you unnecessary stress as the pressure mounts.

I remember losing my temper one day during a marketing offsite because I was imagining another year of the same wastefulness that I had experienced the year before. I started manifesting the aggravation of another lost year of my career, and before I knew it, I was wearing that negative emotion on my sleeve so that everyone could see it. That negativity was highlighted during my annual review, and it cost me a portion of my annual merit increase. Could I have handled it better at the time? Absolutely yes, with one or more of the tools you are about to be introduced to.

This chapter gives you the tools to tap into your positive imagination. Let your inner child out of his or her cage as you have fun with these tips, tools, and techniques.

Remember: Each suggestion will have a key with the letter(s) highlighted in the word LIGHTEN™ to let you know that this tip, tool, or technique applies to that particular topic or topics of the model.

 = Author Uses Personally

 = Shortcut to Implementation

Visualization

(**LIGHTEN**™: **L**ivelihood, **I**magination, **H**ealth, **T**ime, **E**nvironment, and **N**etwork)

Visualization is a powerful form of stress relief using your imagination. By using your mind's creativity, you can quickly put yourself into a more relaxed state. To experiment with this technique, try the following exercise.

 "When I feel stressed at work, I close my eyes and imagine that I am back home in Puerto Rico. I can hear the whisper of the waves. I can feel soft sand under my feet. After one minute, I always feel refreshed."

—YARITZA S., CLIENT

Lighten your day (1 minute):

Stop what you are doing, close your eyes and let your mind go blank. Picture yourself in an environment that is relaxing to you, such as sitting on the beach, floating in a swimming pool, or taking a walk. Imagine yourself interacting with your surroundings. For example, if you imagine yourself on the beach, feel the wind on your face, smell the sea air, or visualize yourself searching for seashells.

You will likely feel a calming sense within the first minute of this exercise, but stay in your relaxing space as long as necessary. Come back to yourself slowly, open your eyes and keep the feelings of relaxation with you.

Remember the Lottery
(LIGHTEN™: **I**magination and **E**nvironment)

This is one of my favorite exercises, and math enthusiasts in particular will get a kick out of this technique.

The next time you are stressing about how difficult life is, remember the lottery.

Of the 115 billion people who have ever lived, about 7 billion people are alive today. That means 108 billion people are dead and will never again have the chance to experience the little things in life that makes life worth living. Being alive means you have already won the lottery.

You are also among the wealthiest people in the entire world. The average world income is $5,000 per year. If you are higher than that, you are in the top 50%. And if you are higher than $50,000 per year, you are in the top 0.5%. You already have more than the majority of people on the planet. On your very worst days, you have to push out your negative and limiting beliefs. You have to remember the lottery because you have already won.[42]

You can remember the lottery for just about anything – having your health, food in the fridge, hair on your head, a roof over you, a car to drive. Any or all of these are part of a positive perspective that does wonders for your stress relief.

Lighten your day (1 minute):

When you wake up in the morning, remember that you have already won the lottery because you have this day to live. Only 7 percent of those who have ever lived on earth currently have that opportunity.

Expect a Magnificent Outcome

(**LIGHTEN**™: **L**ivelihood, **I**magination, **H**ealth, **T**ime, **E**nvironment, and **N**etwork)

This technique is a specific form of visualization. Each morning, before you start or leave for work, set an intention for what you want to happen. It might be as simple as getting to and from work safely, or having a successful meeting with your coworkers, or passing that test you have scheduled for the day.

It really doesn't matter what the intention is, as long as you set the outcome you want. This puts you in the right frame of mind and reduces your perceived stress about what you have planned for the day. What works best for me is setting a daily reminder on my phone for 7:00 a.m. I see that prompt, and I take 30 seconds to say out loud what my magnificent outcome for the day is.

Lighten your day (1 minute):

Set a daily reminder in your phone's calendar that corresponds to the time you typically start or leave work. Put the words "expect a magnificent outcome" as the reminder, and then take a minute to visualize what a magnificent outcome would be for you that day or evening.

Repeating Mantras

(LIGHTEN™: **I**magination and **E**nvironment)

A mantra is a positive word or phrase you say to yourself silently or out loud. It is a good way to stay focused and calm. This technique requires you to close your eyes, think of something motivating or inspiring, and repeat this to yourself whenever you feel like you are losing control. Reminding yourself with the mantra to "pick your battles" or that "this too shall pass" can have a relaxing effect in under one minute.

Mantras can be anything meaningful to you. I often like the simple phrase "thank you" that I chant over and over and over again. This mantra reminds me to have gratitude for what I have, and that whatever is stressing me is not that big a deal in the grand scheme of things.

Lighten your day (1 minute):

Close your eyes and think of your favorite vacation spot, whether you have been there or dreamed about being there. Start repeating quietly to yourself the name of that place for one minute. For example, "Australia. Australia. Australia." After one minute, open your eyes and notice how your stress has reduced.

Don't Try to Control the Uncontrollable
(**LI**GHTEN™: **L**ivelihood, **I**magination, **E**nvironment, and **N**etwork)

Many things we experience are beyond our control, such as traffic, weather, flight delays, the economy, and the behavior of other people. If you are a parent, you especially understand that controlling your kids is a challenging and often futile proposition. Things that are out of your control attract your attention, and by giving those factors your attention you are setting yourself up for stress.

Rather than worrying over things beyond your control, why not focus on the things you can control?

A good technique for helping you with this is the 50 percent rule which states that 50 percent of a challenge is within your control and 50 percent is not. Be 100 percent focused on the proportion of the task you can control. By following this rule, you ensure your contribution is effective before wasting any time, energy, or attention on the 50 percent that isn't within your control. The 50 percent rule puts you in charge.[43]

This mindset also applies to events in the future that have not happened. In other words, you should feel okay about not knowing exactly how things will turn out. Accept the unpredictability of life. Can you imagine how dull life would be if we knew everything that was going to happen? Think of all that is right with your life, control what you can, and embrace ambiguity in the future unknown.[44]

 "I fly for business often, and I used to get stressed about flying. By learning not to try to control the uncontrollable, I don't worry anymore. The only things I can control on the plane is the good music in my headphones and refreshing drinks."

—JOHN B., CLIENT

Lighten your day (1 minute):

Feeling overwhelmed? Honestly ask yourself the question "what can I control?" and then draw a circle.
List what you think you can control about that situation or task inside the circle and what you cannot control outside the circle. The items you can control become your priority, and those that are beyond your control you let go of. This question puts you in charge of power you have, and when you feel more in control, your stress goes down.

Reframe Failing
(**LI**GHTEN™: **L**ivelihood and **I**magination)

When you are progressing forward, you will run into obstacles along the way. But rather than thinking of failure as something negative, consider it part of your education and an investment in your future success. When you fail, it just means it is time to try something another way. In other words, failure is just feedback. When you fail, the world is telling you to take a different approach.

When you think of failure, rather than feedback, you fall into that inner-critic trap discussed in the "Talk to Yourself" technique. We all fail—that's part of life—so how we perceive failure is what separates those who can reduce their stress and those who will continue to pile it on.

In fact, an organization called "The Church of Fail" teaches us to celebrate failures (see the video link provided in the endnotes for more information). During their events, attendees step forward in front of an audience and answer three questions about what they failed at. After they present, they receive a round of applause and are not allowed to step down until the applause has ended. The peculiar feeling that comes from accepting a round of applause, coupled with vulnerability of sharing, leaves a greater mark than if you sat quietly in a room noting you'd made a mistake.[45]

Pretty much everyone who has ever tried anything has cupboards full of botched attempts, rejection letters, and memories of being passed over and ignored. Let's face it, we've all failed. Maybe not on a grand scale, but in some way, shape, or form, we've screwed up.[46] So stop stressing and remember you are part of a very large club. In fact, you could even celebrate your failure with others by attending a local F★★k Up Night (FUN) event in your area. During the event, professionals recount about their worst work screwups and celebrate them to burn off steam and feel better about themselves.[47]

I have not failed. I've just found 10,000 ways that won't work.

—THOMAS A. EDISON, AMERICAN INVENTOR

Lighten your day (1 minute):

If a test, project, interview, or another important effort doesn't go well, don't think of it or yourself as a failure. Rather, consider it feedback on your path to getting better. This will help silence your inner critic and minimize the unnecessary stress that comes with it. If you need more inspiration, Google the term "epic fails." From the results, watch a video or read a short example of someone else who has experienced failure. This will help remind you that it is human nature to fail, and that you must look at your failure as only feedback on your road to succeeding.

Watch an Animal Video
(LIGHTEN™: Imagination)

Okay, I admit it: When I am on social media, particularly Facebook, I often look at short length animal videos that give me a chuckle. Interestingly, there is research that proves that these videos can help reduce your stress.

In an innovative study, Deborah Wells examined whether merely looking at a video of an animal can have the same type of calming and restorative effects as those created by being in its company. Compared to the two control conditions (a video of humans and a blank screen), all three animal videos (one each of a bird, fish, and primate) made the participants feel much more relaxed, reducing their heart rate and blood pressure in the process—similar to what would be found had the animals been real.[48]

Lighten your day (1 minute):

Google "funny animal videos" and take a minute or two to unwind and get a laugh. If you think you might not get back to work, set an alarm as a reminder to get back to your tasks.

Unsubscribe from Mailing Lists
(**LI**GHTEN™: **L**ivelihood, **I**magination, and **T**ime)

There is only so much information we can take in on a daily basis, yet we are exposed to so many messages. Studies show that the average consumer is exposed to up to 10,000 brand messages a day, and that number is growing rapidly. Consumers switch between device screens up to 21 times an hour, and the average person's attention span is now just eight seconds.[49]

To reduce the amount of unnecessary information you're subjected to, take a minute to unsubscribe from newsletters, blogs, podcasts, and marketing emails you're no longer interested in. This makes it easier to focus on what truly matters and not get stuck in information overload and analysis paralysis.[50]

Lighten your day (1 minute):

For any newsletter, podcast, or webinar invite that is not of interest to you, click the unsubscribe link. You will remove future distractions from more important information and save time by being more focused.

The Declipse Habit

(L**I**GHT**EN**™: **I**magination, **E**nvironment, and **N**etwork)

Another variation of the visualization technique, this tool will help you move from a stressful state of agitation to a calmer state of insight. When we have a strong emotion, it behaves (metaphorically) like an eclipse, inadvertently creating a blind spot in our decision-making and blocking access to an alternative perspective that could bring wisdom or insight. The eclipse generates the tension of something unresolved. The agitated mind yearns for a "declipse," to get past the stuck place of an eclipse and find resolution and balance.[51]

To give this tool a try, follow the steps below.

Lighten your day (5 minutes):

1. *Focus on your agitated feeling.*

2. *Ask the agitation, "What costume do you want to wear?" or "What do you look like?"*

3. *Allow your creative mind to serve up an image of what's behind your feeling. As an example, the image could be of a fireman trying to put out a fire.*

4. *Clear your mind to a still place.*

5. *Allow your creative mind to serve up an image of an antidote. For example, the antidote to the fireman could be snow falling from the sky that puts out the fire.*

6. *Allow this opposite energy to "declipse" the agitation that was "eclipsing" your wisdom.*

7. *Become aware of the wisdom and insights that show up after the agitation has moved aside.*

Meditation

(LIGHTEN™: Imagination, Genius, Health, and Environment)

Meditation is a practice of focusing your mind on a particular object, thought, or activity to achieve a mentally clear and emotionally calm state. It is one of the most well-known "calming" activities and has been clinically proven to decrease mood disturbance and stress symptoms in both male and female patients.[52]

Meditation apps, such as The Mindfulness App, HeadSpace, and Calm, are becoming more popular and have also shown to be successful in reducing stress.[53] Many of the apps have a free introductory program to allow you to test it and see if it works for you before buying.

If you prefer not to rely on technology to help you meditate, follow the simple process below.[54]

Lighten your day (5 minutes):

1. *Find a comfortable, quiet spot to meditate. Sit on the floor or in a comfortable chair. Avoid meditating on your bed at first because you'll be more likely to doze off in the middle of your practice.*

2. *Contrary to popular belief, you don't have to learn how to shut off your brain if you want to meditate. Instead, meditating regularly allows you to have an open dialogue with yourself without judgment and emotional reaction. When you notice your mind wandering, just bring it back into focus.*

3. *Inhale to the count of four, then hold your breath for seven beats. Exhale for four more seconds. As you release your breath, feel the air make its way out of your lungs and nose and concentrate on the lightness in your chest. On each inhale and exhale, count for one breath. Repeat as needed.*

Minimize Expectations
(**LI**GHTEN™: **L**ivelihood, **I**magination, and **N**etwork)

All of us like to get things done, and those of us who are achievement-oriented tend to overdeliver whenever possible. We set very high expectations for ourselves and, in the process, pile on the pressure to provide what we promised. But what happens when we don't deliver? The real problem is expectation: the stress caused when we think we've let others down.

Falling short of expectations causes us unhappiness. We are constantly doing this to ourselves. This leads to anxiety, feeling overwhelmed, and/or a lack of trust in ourselves—this is the real damage. It hurts everything we want to do, making it more likely that we just give up, because we have limiting beliefs.

The answer is to hold less tightly to our ideals. Become aware of our own and others' expectations and give yourself permission to ease up on yourself. Remember: you are only human.

If you failed to deliver, let go of the useless guilt and self-criticism. Instead, see what held you back from meeting your intention. Make a deliberate change in your environment so that it won't keep holding you back. Set another intention, and don't cling to it. Repeat, over and over.[55]

To take it one step further, consider redefining your metrics (how you measure success). Do not choose to measure yourself as a rising star or an undiscovered genius, a tragic victim, or dismal failure. Instead, measure yourself by more mundane identities: a student, a partner, a friend, a creator.[56] Minimizing expectations this way allows you to be kind to yourself, reducing your stress in the process.

Lighten your day (10 minutes):

Think back to the last time you didn't live up to your expectation. List out all the reasons that got in the way from you meeting your intention. Objectively evaluate those reasons, focusing on those within your control that you could have eliminated. This clarity will help you re-evaluate the situation and help you set more realistic expectations of yourself to ensure future success.

S.T.O.P. Method

(**LIGHTEN**™: **L**ivelihood, **I**magination, **H**ealth, and **N**etwork)

We've all been in a stressful situation when we lose our temper and say something we later wish we hadn't said, and then we worry over the ramifications of our actions.

Fortunately, there is a solution to avoid this from happening in the future, and it's called the S.T.O.P. method:[57]

- **S**top what you are doing when you feel your emotions being triggered, and excuse yourself from the situation.
- **T**ake a few deep breaths.
- **O**bserve what is going on inside your mind and body—your thoughts, emotions and physical response.
- **P**roceed once you have processed your physical and mental reaction to the situation.

After you have completed the S.T.O.P. method, consider talking to a friend, getting a cup of tea, or taking a short walk before returning to the scene of the crime. You will be refreshed and thinking more rationally.

Lighten your day (10 minutes):

Close your eyes and think back to a time when you remember feeling your blood boiling in a situation with someone else. Visualize yourself stopping and excusing yourself from the situation, taking three deep breaths, and assessing how your body and mind were reacting. By reflecting on why this person got under your skin, you provide yourself insight so that you go back to the situation feeling calmer. Note that when you use this tool in a live situation, you can take a short walk to help you further de-stress, especially if you need a little extra time to process and calm yourself.

Play Fact or Fiction

(**LIG**HTEN™: **I**magination and **G**enius)

Do you have a tendency to worry about things that may not be true? For example, what if on a Monday you realize your coworkers are sneezing and coughing around you, and you have tickets to a Broadway show on Friday. You won't necessarily catch whatever they have, but if you are getting anxious, playing fact or fiction might help reduce your stress.

On a piece of paper, draw four columns. On the far left, write the worry you're having. In the next column identify whether it is fact or fiction and if there's any real evidence to support your belief. Then write an alternative way of thinking, and finally, think about whether the original thought was helpful or not.

So, in the example of worrying you may miss the Broadway show if you get sick:

> Column 1. I'm worried I'll get sick and have to miss the show on Friday.
>
> Column 2. I'm not sick now, so the thought is unwarranted and fiction.

Column 3. I'll make sure I take care of myself and get proper rest so I am healthy for my show.

Column 4. (After the event) I didn't get sick, and I made it to the show. My worries were needless and didn't affect my health.[58]

If you play fact or fiction on a few issues that are making you anxious, you will start to train your brain to not worry so much.

 "I am a hypochondriac and am constantly worried about getting sick before vacation. The more I worried, the sicker I would feel, making me stress even more. Playing fact or fiction helped me to let go of my anxiety and I now feel better even when I'm not on vacation!"

—PETER P., CLIENT

Lighten your day (10-15 minutes):

Are you anxious and stressed about a future event? Give the following process a try:

1. *Draw four columns on a piece of paper, with the first column naming your worry.*

2. *In the second column, write down any evidence that supports your worry.*

3. *In the third column, write down an alternative way of dealing with the worry.*

4. *In the fourth column, write down evidence that can support your alternative thought process.*

5. *Compare the columns and reflect, especially after the event, to see whether your stress was warranted.*

Journaling
(**LIGHTEN**™: **L**ivelihood, **I**magination, **G**enius, and **N**etwork)

If you are feeling overwhelmed, you may need to just get it all out of your head. Journaling allows you to clarify your thoughts and feelings, thereby gaining valuable self-knowledge. It's also a good problem-solving tool because, oftentimes, you can hash out a problem and come up with solutions more easily on paper. As a stress management and self-exploration tool, journaling works best when done consistently, but even occasional, sporadic journaling can be stress relieving, especially if it incorporates gratitude or emotional processing.[59]

Journaling can also help you immediately before a stressful event like taking a test. In one study, students highly anxious about taking tests who wrote down their thoughts beforehand received an average grade of B+. They were compared with the highly anxious students who didn't write and received an average grade of B-. Writing about their worries for 10 minutes before an upcoming exam leveled the playing field such that those students who usually got most anxious during exams were able to overcome their fears and perform up to their potential.[60]

Lighten your day (15-30 minutes):

Sit in a quiet place with a paper and pen and start writing everything you have been through during the stressful situation. Include the things that bothered you, what you are grateful for, your hopes, feelings and fears. Once you have it all down on paper, look over your notes and figure out what you can take control of right now. Refer to the "Don't Try to Control the Uncontrollable" technique if you need a refresher. This process will help reduce the burden of your worry.

Create Your Ideal Day

(**LI**GH**TE**N™: **L**ivelihood, **I**magination, **T**ime, and **E**nvironment)

Have you ever looked up at the clock and wondered where your day has gone? That's what happens when you don't have a good grasp of how you would like your day to go in a perfect world. Fortunately, there is a technique that might help you.

By comparing your ideal day to your typical day, you can see gaps that you can help address to make your typical day closer to what your ideal day could be. All you have to do is describe your experiences in both days to identify gaps that you need to address.

Post the description of your ideal day on your wall and revisit/revise it as needed. It gives you a clearer picture and enables you to act intentionally in the interest of creating your model day.[61] And when you can create your ideal day, you are far less likely to get stressed.

Lighten your day (15-30 minutes):

1. *Write down what an ideal day at work would look like for you. What would you do (or not do)? What would you accomplish? How would you describe your feelings, and your experience?*

2. *On a separate page, write down what your typical day looks like (including your feelings and experience).*

3. *Compare your ideal day to your typical day and note the gaps.*

4. *Post your ideal day up on your wall and revisit/revise it as needed. Over time you should notice that you are gaining back control of your day, and as a result you should be less stressed.*

Coloring or Doodling

(LIGHTEN™: Imagination and Genius)

Thinking back to your school days, you can probably remember coloring or doodling while one of your teachers droned on about a boring subject. This activity helped you pass the time while also listening somewhat to what was being said. It was an early form of multitasking that many of us have carried into our adult lives full of dull meetings.

Coloring offers an escape to all the stress and responsibilities of adult life without having to spend a lot of money or time on the activity. Even if you only have a few minutes to spare each day, carving out the time for this quiet activity can make a big difference in your mindset and stress levels.

Studies have proven the benefits of adult coloring books. First of all, coloring helps you detach from your worries temporarily because you're focused on the task at hand. The studies also show an increase in mindfulness and decrease in anxiety, which is the whole point of the exercise.[62]

If you like freehand doodling or drawing, a simple sketch pad and pencil will work. If you prefer just to color, there are a lot of adult coloring books available online or in bookstores. You can color animals, Disney characters or other shapes. If bad words don't bother you, consider books that have sassy and/or offensive comments to make you laugh or smile as you relax into your coloring activity. One of the best-known adult language set of coloring books can be found at **sashaohara.com.**

Lighten your day (15-30 minutes):

Google "adult coloring books" and order a book that looks appealing to you. Also buy a set of coloring pens if you don't already have them. Once you receive your coloring book, dedicate 15-30 minutes to coloring whenever you feel your stress level is high and you need a mental break. Do it in a place where you won't be distracted, breathe deeply when you color, and put on some music you like if that helps create the right environment.

Allow Yourself to Be Bored

(LIGHTE**N**™: **L**ivelihood, **I**magination, **H**ealth, **T**ime, and **E**nvironment)

This one is a tough one if you are an overachiever like me, but who doesn't like a challenge? Allow yourself to be bored, even for an hour or less. If you don't fight it, the feelings of boredom will be replaced with feelings of peace. And after a little practice, you will learn to relax.

Much of our anxiety and inner struggle stems from our busy, overactive minds always needing something to focus on and always wondering "what's next?" The beauty of doing nothing is that it teaches you to clear your mind and relax. It allows your mind the freedom to "not know," for a brief period of time.

Just like your body, your mind needs an occasional break from its hectic routine. When you allow your mind to take a break, it comes back stronger, sharper, more focused and creative. When you allow yourself to be bored, it takes an enormous amount of pressure off you to be performing and doing something every second of every day.[63]

So, go ahead and be bored. Yawn if you need to and notice your stress start to subside.

 "My favorite way to be bored is to go float in a water chamber. There is no music, no noise, no nothing except your thoughts. I let my mind wander just like I was meditating, but with the added benefit that I'm floating effortlessly in water."

—ADAM S., CLIENT

72

Lighten your day (30-60 minutes):

When a slot in your busy day unexpectedly opens, resist the temptation of filling it with other work or chores. Instead, pour yourself a hot beverage and relax with your own thoughts, even if it's just for a few minutes. Your mind needs a break from sprinting just like your body would.

Read a Good Book

(LIGHTEN™: **I**magination, **T**ime, and **E**nvironment)

Yes, I know this tip is not very insightful! However, if I didn't include it, people would say it was an oversight. So, as with exercise, good nutrition, and a few other obvious suggestions, reading a good book needs to be included as a tool.

It can be tough to find time in the day to read just because you want to. And your environment can be a challenge as well. When you finally make it back home after a day at work, head to a room where you can enjoy reading in silence. If your home is loud because the kids are running around or someone's blasting music outside your apartment, consider heading to a local library or sitting in a park with a good book before the sun goes down.

The key is that you don't have to spend a long time reading. You could just read ten pages a day. If that proves challenging to your schedule or environment, consider listening to an audiobook on your commute. Whatever solution you choose, the fact that you are reading a book for your own pleasure will help with your overall stress level.

> **Lighten your day (30-60 minutes):**
>
> *Is there a book you have been wanting to read, but haven't been able to get around to it because of your busy schedule? Read just ten pages a day or get the audiobook and listen to it on your commute. Taking this personal time will do wonders for your stress relief efforts and improve your knowledge.*

Hobbies

(L**I**GHTE**N**™: **I**magination and **N**etwork)

Use your visualization skills and think back to when you were a child. Do you remember what you did with your free time? Play outside? Read books? Watch movies? Draw and/or create art? Whatever it was, you did it because you liked doing it and it brought you joy.

Now ask yourself when was the last time you did one of those things you enjoyed as a kid? If you are burning the candle at both ends, chances are it's been too long. Or what about a hobby you started as an adult that was pushed aside when your free time became scarce?

Whatever that hobby was, you were doing it because your "inner child" (the little kid inside all of us) wanted to do it, and now you may be feeling anxiety because you are not being true to yourself. Consider scheduling just an hour each week to reconnect with this hobby you have missed. Your inner child will thank you.

"Painting makes me forget about my everyday stress and problems. It makes me happy, just like when I was a little girl."

—Veronica G., client

Lighten your day (1 hour):

Pick an activity you fondly remember doing as a child or younger adult. Block an hour out this weekend to do that activity. If it still brings you joy, block out an hour every weekend for this activity. Involve some friends or family in your hobby, if appropriate, to spread the joy.

Discover Your Personality

(L**I**GHTE**N**™: **I**magination and **N**etwork)

Understanding what your preferences are in certain situations, and how your personality interacts with others, can be quite beneficial to helping you minimize unnecessary stress. Behavior tests, only if you are completely honest in your responses, can give you an accurate description of who you are and why you do things the way you do. You can also learn what really drives, inspires, and worries other types of personalities, helping you build more meaningful relationships.

Two of my favorite behavior tools are the following:

- 16 Personalities. This is a free test based on the Myers-Briggs (**myersbriggs.org**) model. This is great for helping you determine your preferable working style and those within your work team (assuming they all take the test and share their profiles). As an example, I am an ENFJ: a natural born leader. You can take the test by visiting **16personalities.com**.

- Personality Colors. This test and book are great tools to help you communicate with your significant other by understanding what is important to both of you. I found that my temperament is a cross between Orange ("let's all get along") and Green ("let's experience it all"). Search for the book *Love...What's Personality Got to Do With It?* by Carol Ritberger PhD.

Whether you want to communicate better at work or at home, these two tools can be a great start for you.

Lighten your day (1 hour):

Take one or both of the tests listed above and share your results with your coworkers and/or significant other. Encourage them to do the same in the spirit of improving communication and avoiding unnecessary stress that occurs when personalities clash.

Create Your Joy List
(**LIGHTEN**™: **L**ivelihood, **I**magination, **G**enius, **H**ealth, **T**ime, **E**nvironment, and **N**etwork)

We've all had those days we just want to forget. Nothing seemed to go right, and the more we stressed about things, the more things snowballed—am I right? It's easy in those situations to get down, so this is an easy and fun tip to get your mindset back on a positive track.

Create a huge list of what your sources of happiness and joy are; have as many resources to draw on as you possibly can. Your list is unique to you, there is no right or wrong way to feel joy: pictures, songs, nature, comedy, you name it. Whatever works for you.[64] My list includes watching movies with my wife, hiking, attending/watching San Jose Sharks games with my kids, and petting my cat. It also includes the sound of whoopee cushions, funny jokes, favorite music, and connecting with my friends. I could go on, but you get the point: your list can have anything on it that makes you smile.

Your sources of joy will bring you back into alignment whenever you've strayed from your path and don't feel good. Reflecting on the list for just one minute when times are tough will help your stress level come down.

> **Lighten your day (1 hour):**
>
> *Type out or write down 10-20 things that bring you joy. Take a picture of this list with your phone. Any time you feel stressed and/or depressed, take a minute to refer to this list and reflect on why one or more of these items makes you smile. You should notice your stress level reducing as you review your list.*

Vision Board or Binder

(**LIGHTEN**™: **L**ivelihood, **I**magination, **G**enius, **H**ealth, **E**nvironment, and **N**etwork)

This isn't a quick exercise, but it is an easy and fun one. Creating a vision board or binder allows you the opportunity to reflect on what you want when things are not going your way.

You start by writing down what you want in life. For me, that included a healthy body, a career in which I make a difference, economic security, travel opportunities, wonderful family relationships, and a beautiful home.

Let me caution you, though: don't focus just on acquiring "things." Acquiring stuff (bigger houses, fancier cars, etc.) causes anxiety because you have to keep working hard to maintain the costs of supporting these new acquisitions. This situation was one of the main culprits that lead to my divorce (and additional stress, as anyone who has been through a divorce can attest).

Research has shown that material things don't make you happy. People living in extreme poverty experience a significant increase in happiness when their financial circumstances improve, but it drops off quickly above $20,000 in annual income. When you make a habit of chasing things, you are likely to become unhappy. Why? Because beyond the disappointment you experience once you get them, you discover that you've gained them at the expense of the real things that bring you joy such as friends, family, and hobbies.[65]

Once you have your list, start collecting a bunch of images, either printed from the internet or from old magazines, and then decide where it will live. If you have space on your wall, pin up your vision board, or to have it handy, create a vision binder to carry around. Once you decide your format, start organizing your images on your board or your binder until you have enough images to reinforce what you are striving for.

Use your vision board/binder any time work gets challenging, or when experiencing any other stressful situation. Your vision board/binder will remind you of why you are working so hard and where you ultimately want to go, and it will have a calming effect on your demeanor.

Lighten your day (3 hours):

Write a list of what you would like to experience in life, focusing not just on material things. Once you have that list, start searching the internet for images that match those items you have listed. Save those images, and then block a few hours out of your week to arrange those images on a board or in a binder that you can refer to any time you need a diversion from your stress and a reminder of what you are working towards.

Write Your Own Eulogy

(**LI**GHTEN™: **L**ivelihood, **I**magination, **H**ealth, **T**ime, and **N**etwork)

What a sad ending to your life it would be to be lying on your death bed worrying over a decision that you did or didn't make. If there is a better reality check than this, I can't imagine what it would be. I certainly know I won't regret that I didn't spend an additional hour a day working.

When we write about how we'd like to be remembered, we can examine our priorities and goals from a broader perspective. It helps remind us of what truly matters in our life, and whether our time spent is in proper alignment with our true self.

The following technique can be quite enlightening.[66]

Lighten your day (4 hours):

Draft two eulogies to be read at your funeral. The first one should be as if you were to have died today. Visualize the first three rows and be brutally honest about your impact on those people who are likely your closest friends and family, compared to the others who are sitting in rows 10 through 20 (your acquaintances, clients and customers).

Now write the second eulogy that encompasses all your future achievements, keeping in mind the same people in those first three rows. Compare the two to re-evaluate how you are spending your time and the decisions you are making. When you are true to yourself, you start releasing the anxiety caused by the expectations of others who don't matter as much.

Reflection Point

Now that we are at the end of this chapter, which stress-relief tool did you like best? What was it about the tool you liked? Making notes to yourself below will help commit what you've learned to memory:

The stress-relief tool I like best:

I will use this tool specifically for:

The one that worked best for you should be bookmarked so you can easily refer to it in the future. You can also share it with your friends and family as a way of giving back to your community. There are also video-instruction stress-relief tools available for you to review and share by visiting my blog at **PeteAlexander.com**.

Remember that marketing offsite I mentioned at the beginning of the chapter? In hindsight, as soon as I noticed my temper rising, I should have excused myself from the meeting and found a quiet place to visualize myself hiking in nature with the sun on my face and the fresh air breathing in and out of my body. I would have calmed myself down in a short amount of time and been able to return to the meeting more grounded. I also would have avoided a lot of self-imposed negative energy I was manifesting, and that negative mark on my annual review would have been avoided.

Now I use visualization on a regular basis, and it has become a habit. And once you have a habit formed, you have tapped into the power of your unconscious mind, which is the subject of our next chapter.

The true sign of intelligence is not knowledge but imagination.

—ALBERT EINSTEIN, GERMAN PHYSICIST

CHAPTER 5

GENIUS—
Tips, Tools, and Techniques
for Tapping into the Power of
Your Unconscious

*You can't calm the storm, so stop trying. What
you can do is calm yourself. The storm will pass.*

—TIMBER HAWKEYE, AMERICAN AUTHOR

As discussed previously, most stress is of the mental variety, so
it's imperative that you find stress-relief tools that calm your
mind. And while the imagination part of your active mind is
important, even more important will be your ability to get in touch with
your unconscious mind that runs on autopilot and is in charge of your
memories, habits, beliefs, likes, and dislikes. The unconscious mind also
stores emotional baggage, i.e., the feelings you have about your past and
the things that have happened to you, which often have a negative effect
on your behavior and attitudes.

The majority of us come with some emotional baggage from negative
life events that results in limiting beliefs about our abilities. My emotional

baggage comes primarily from being brought up in a dysfunctional, alcoholic household. The PTSD as a result of that environment can last a lifetime if one doesn't choose to overcome that trauma.

Case in point. One of my clients is a successful manager in the entertainment industry. Even though she has 12 people reporting to her and is excellent at her job, she was her own worst enemy when it came to her confidence. She would allow those who reported to her to be disrespectful and aloof. Through discovery, we determined that the primary source of her problem was a low self-worth that stemmed from childhood. I'll detail what we did together to address that issue later in this chapter.

The reality is that real and sustained change happens on the unconscious level. Our active mind can say "yes," but if our unconscious mind is not aligned, permanent change isn't going to happen. Therefore, the tips, tools, and techniques included in this chapter are designed to help align yourself with your active and unconscious minds.

Remember: *Each suggestion will have a key with the letter(s) highlighted in the word LIGHTEN™ to let you know that this tip, tool, or technique applies to that particular topic or topics of the model.*

 = *Author Uses Personally*

 = *Shortcut to Implementation*

Avoid Ruminating
(**LIGH**TEN™: **I**magination, **G**enius, and **H**ealth)

The process of repeatedly thinking about events in the past or future and attaching negative emotions to it is called rumination. We've all done it. We think about how we failed at something and continuously beat ourselves up about it. Or we create unnecessary anxiety and stress thinking negatively about a future event.

Maybe it is pressure you are feeling at work or at home (or both). Well, here is another important learning moment for you: pressure does **NOT** equal stress.[67]

Pressure is an external demand on your environment, and everyone has it. However, to convert pressure into stress you must ruminate about it. Those who don't ruminate are much less stressed. Sure, you have to do some rumination about what happened in the past (e.g., reflecting on lessons learned), but if you keep it positive and constructive, it will not add to your stress.

Ruminating about future events is just as bad as ruminating in the past. If you are working on something very important, constantly reminding yourself of the high stakes will impede your performance because instead of being motivating, these thoughts are likely to increase anxiety and undermine your confidence. Research shows that reminding yourself how unimportant the event is in the big scheme of things is a better tactic to keep you from stressing out.[68]

Lighten your day (1 minute):

When you are ruminating on a troubling thought, put your repetitive belief in perspective. Remember that your perception is your reality, but by understanding that your troubling thought might not be accurate, you will realize the negative belief is not worth the energy involved. Think of what is troubling you and how it fits in to your life 5 months or 5 years from now to minimize its true impact and whether it is worth your worry.

Ask the Pendulum
(LIGHTEN™: Imagination and Genius)

Remember Disney's *Snow White* when the wicked queen asks, *"Mirror, mirror on the wall, who's the fairest one of all?"*? Well, a magic mirror doesn't exist, but something almost as good does. It's called a pendulum, and you can use one to ask yes or no questions to help you make a decision that is causing you stress.

This process can be used for both small and large decisions, although the larger and more troublesome the decision, the more likely the pendulum will swing with a clear answer. The trick is to ask very specific yes or no questions. For example, you could rephrase the question "should I quit my job?" to "should I quit my job tomorrow (or next week, month, etc.)?" Your body and mind will work together in harmony to help you get clarity on your decision at hand. Chances are you know what the right decision is; the pendulum process simply helps confirm it.

While this might come across as a bit "woo-woo," the fact that your body and mind align to help you make decisions is the bottomline benefit of this process. In other words, making a decision provides you with stress relief.

Try this process with a pendant you already have that has some weight to it, and if it works for you, you can go online and buy a pendulum that you can dedicate for future questions.

"I have a hard time making decisions,
so my pendulum is my go-to tool. I use it
to make big decisions, like whether to leave
my job, and everyday decisions, like what to
wear when I go out on a date. It's crazy, but
it's never failed to lead me to the
right decision."

—Alice C., client

Lighten your day (1 minute):

Take a pendant on a chain and hold it in one hand, letting it hang down vertically. Make sure it is steady, and then ask "pendulum, show me yes" and watch to see if the pendant moves in a particular direction. If you see a slight movement, you can ask it to "amplify." Do the same process for "no," calibrating the pendant for both yes and no.

You are now ready to ask the pendulum yes or no answers. Be specific in your questions, otherwise you won't get the answer you are looking for. Coming to a decision will help relieve your stress.

Your Perception Is Your Reality

(**LIGHTEN**™: **L**ivelihood, **I**magination, **G**enius, **H**ealth, **T**ime, **E**nvironment, and **N**etwork)

Have you ever gotten stressed just thinking about a particular situation, only to find out later it was no big deal? This used to happen to me all the time. More recently, I was enlightened to the fact that how we perceive the world around us becomes our reality, even if that reality is indeed false.

For example, if we think something is going to be stressful, we manifest that anxiety internally and we exert energy to deal with that negative thought without knowing the true facts. What we have done is change our actions based on what we think might be the outcome, when the situation may not be stressful at all.

Another example of this phenomenon is when you are running late. Have you noticed that when you are rushing, you are more likely to hit red lights instead of green lights? Or that you can't find your car keys, wallet, etc. when you know you need to be leaving? Every negative reaction we have to the fact that we are running late adds to our anxiety, and we become frazzled with each minute more that we are delayed.

Conversely, "perception is reality" also works when there is a positive in your life. For example, if you are in the market for a new car, or just bought one, have you noticed that you see more of that same make and model than you did before? It isn't that more people are magically driving that model, it's that you now notice those vehicles on the road more because your perception has changed.

It's not stress that kills us, it is our reaction to it.

—HANS SELYE, CANADIAN SCIENTIST

> **Lighten your day (1 minute):**
>
> *When a problem occurs that you perceive as a big deal, ask yourself the following question: will this matter 5 years from now? Or even 5 weeks from now? Honesty think about that for a minute and you will notice your stress level coming way down as your perception likely changes as reality sets in.*

Talk to Yourself

(LIGHTEN™: Imagination and Genius)

I'll give you one guess what your biggest challenge is. Yep, it's you. We all have that inner critic inside of us, that voice that constantly is putting us down and telling us we are not good enough. The critical inner voice is formed out of painful early life experiences in which we witnessed or experienced hurtful attitudes toward us or those close to us. As we grow up, we unconsciously adopt and integrate this pattern of destructive thoughts toward ourselves and others.[69]

Rather than listening to negative self-talk, be proactive and start talking to yourself in a more constructive way. It's as simple as tweaking the way you speak to yourself. Asking ourselves questions rather than issuing commands is a much more effective way to create change.

When you catch your inner critic flinging accusations, think, *how can I turn this statement into a question?* Asking questions encourages greater exploration and opens up more possibilities. Here are some examples: Am I willing to do what it takes? When have I done this before? What if [insert worst case scenario] happens? How can I...? This type of self-inquiry powers up problem-solving areas of the brain, helping you tap into your innate creativity. You're able to greet negative thoughts with curiosity instead of fear, thus minimizing the unnecessary stress we put on ourselves.[70]

> **Lighten your day (1 minute):**
>
> When you hear your inner critic talking negatively, ask yourself questions to help you snap out of that negative state. A good one to ask is "what do I really care about?" because it will get you thinking about what's important to you and relieve your stress in the process.

Affirmations

(L**IGH**TEN™: **I**magination, **G**enius, and **H**ealth)

Affirmations are simple statements designed to flood your brain with positive self-talk to overcome your inner critic (refer to the "Talk to Yourself" technique for a refresher) and get you into a more upbeat, stress-free state. To employ this tip, all you need to do is read an affirmation you like over and over again; just Google "positive affirmations" to find a list that appeals to you.

Another option is to use a mobile phone app, like Think Up (**https://thinkup.me/**) to help you overcome challenges. You record affirmations in your own voice and listen to them just like you would your favorite music.

To improve the effectiveness, consider speaking your affirmation out loud as you look at yourself in the mirror. Regardless of how you use them, affirmations can be helpful to use right before you have a stressful event such as an important meeting or presentation.

👍 "When I started working with Professor Alexander, I placed positive sticky notes with affirmations on the edge of my bathroom mirror. It has helped me to love myself and to start the day with a positive thought."

—CHRIS A., CLIENT

> **Lighten your day (1 minute):**
>
> *Search Google for a positive affirmation that resonates with you. Copy it into your phone where you have easy access to it. Read that affirmation repeatedly for one minute to help calm your mind and reduce your stress level.*

Reframe Your Fear

(**LIG**HTEN™: **I**magination and **G**enius)

Fear is an emotional response to an actual threat, and it's a fundamental survival mechanism that dates back to the Stone Age, when survival from predators was of primary concern. Fear is also a true emotional response when we're about to lose someone or something that's important to us. And it's not just about our personal safety: we can fear the loss of a loved one to illness, or our home to foreclosure.

The solution to your fear may just be reframing it. Do you know what the acronym F.E.A.R. stands for? False Evidence Appearing Real. It is an illusion, something we fabricate in our own minds that feels real. It's a fairy tale we tell ourselves that keeps us from doing what we really want.[71]

The best way to move out of your fear is to get out of your comfort zone and visualize what it would be like to overcome your fear. Is there a clear path to getting there? Ask yourself what you would attempt if you knew you could not fail.[72] You might surprise yourself with what your active and unconscious mind comes up with.

If that doesn't work, try a slightly different approach. Ask yourself, "what is the worst that can happen?" And then follow up with "and then what?" "Okay, and then what?" and "Okay, and then what?" By going through this process of following a line of thought, you may find that the particular fear no longer has a hold on you.[73]

> **Lighten your day (1 minute):**
>
> Next time you are fearful of trying something new, ask yourself, "What would I attempt to do if I knew I could not fail?" Notice whether your anxiety reduces as you ponder the answer.

Avoid the Victim Mentality

(**LIG**HTEN™: **I**magination and **G**enius)

This was another important moment for me in my quest to reduce my stress. The severe family dysfunction I experienced as a child turned me into an angry young adult who liked to blame others for everything: my boss, my parents, family, and friends. Fortunately, I discovered a 12-step program called Adult Children of Alcoholic and Dysfunctional Families (ACoA) which taught me to take responsibility for my own actions and become my own loving parent.[74] I have been an active member of this program since 1990.

I've also been inspired by Regina Hartley's presentation about Scrappers. Scrappers reframe childhood Post Traumatic Stress Disorder (PTSD) as Post Traumatic Success Decision. They are driven by the belief that the only person they can change is themselves. They figure if they can survive their upbringing, the challenges of business are a piece of cake.[75]

Everyone has a story of struggle to share. Some people define themselves by it; others act in spite of it. The important thing to remember is that your past will only be your future if you carry it there. You can take action at any time to change your attitude, especially if you ask yourself if there is anyone worse off than you. If you answer this question honestly, chances are your perspective will change.

> **_Lighten your day (1 minute):_**
>
> _When you start feeling sorry for yourself, ask yourself, "Is there anyone on the planet having it worse than me right now?" Take your answer to heart, pick yourself back up, and notice your outlook improving and your stress level reducing._

It's Either HELL YES! or No

(**LIG**HTEN™: **I**magination and **G**enius)

If you are stressing over making a difficult decision, consider putting the resolution to an extreme test. If you feel total and utter conviction to do something (HELL YEAH!), then the answer is yes. Anything less gets a thumbs down.[76]

This simplifies your decision-making process and eliminates lingering stress. If you are concerned about trying this technique with a big decision, try it with a minor decision first and work your way up to the more important decisions as your confidence grows.

 "When we were buying our new home, I looked at my husband and asked him, 'Is it a Hell yes?' And it was!"

—DEBORAH D., CLIENT

> **_Lighten your day (1 minute):_**
>
> _Struggling with a decision that needs to be made? Expedite the process by resolving that anything less than you answering, "Hell Yes!" should be a no. Your stress will go down with the definitive decision._

Label Your Stress

(**LIG**HTEN™: **I**magination and **G**enius)

The word stress is used generically to describe any kind of anxiety, agitation, anger, fear, guilt, or sadness we are feeling. However, if we simply describe the emotion that is fueling our stress in a few words, it will help reduce the charge of the emotion.[77]

For example, when I feel that someone has let me down (oh those dreaded expectations), instead of thinking/saying "I feel disappointed" I describe it in a few more words such as "I feel disappointed because ..." By describing my emotions with a little more detail, this identification process helps me to start relaxing.

Lighten your day (1 minute):

Think about the last time you were feeling stressed and identify the emotion you were feeling. Once you have that emotion identified, describe it with a little more detail, such as: "I felt angry because..." This simple process of self-awareness can have a calming effect on your system and will serve you well as you are experiencing stress.

Hakalau

(**LIG**HTEN™: **L**ivelihood, **I**magination, **G**enius, and **E**nvironment)

If you get anxiety before giving an important presentation, this tool is for you. Hakalau is a light meditation suited for calming you before you need to present. It originates from the ancient Hawaiian Huna system called "the walking meditation of the *kahuna*" because the *kahuna* (a wise man or shaman) who practiced it were able to walk around and function while remaining in the state. There are five steps to this form of meditation:[78]

1. Pick a spot on the wall to look at, preferably above eye level. Your field of vision should bump up against your eyebrows, but not so high as to cut off the field of vision.

2. As you stare at this spot, just let your mind go loose, and focus all your attention on the spot.

3. Notice that within a matter of moments, your vision begins to spread out, and you see more in the peripheral than you do in the central part of your vision.

4. Now pay attention to the peripheral. In fact, pay more attention to the peripheral than to the central part of your vision.

5. Stay in this state for as long as you can. Notice how it feels.

You are now calmer and more aware of your surroundings, and you are now more present and more ready to give a great presentation. As you practice Hakalau more and more, you will find that it can help dissipate your stress in other situations, like conflict management with your peers and/or loved ones.

Lighten your day (5 minutes):

When you have to speak in front of an audience, get to the room early before everyone arrives. Stand where you will be presenting and follow the five steps above. You will be more calm, present, and centered for you and your audience.

Find Something Nostalgic

(LIGHTEN™: Genius)

There is a specialty candy shop not far from where I live, and every time I walk in there, I'm reminded of my favorite childhood treats. As soon as I pick up one of those candies and read the label, I immediately get nostalgic. Interestingly, those proficient at reminiscing—looking back on happy times, rekindling joy from happy memories—are best able to buffer stress.[79]

Is there an old toy you have from your childhood sitting in a box waiting to comfort you? Maybe it is an old photo album you haven't looked through in years. Or maybe you just need a bite of your favorite childhood candy. You can probably find anything that brings up positive nostalgia for you simply by Googling it.

Lighten your day (5 minutes):

When stress starts building inside of you, think about something you liked from your childhood—a toy, TV show, snack, etc. Google that memory and see what pops up. You might see an old commercial, an image, hear a jingle, or read a slogan. Whatever it is, take a few minutes and reminisce about the joy that item brought to you in the past. And if you crave that item, treat yourself if it is still available to be purchased.

Listen to Music

(LIGHTEN™: Imagination, Genius, Time, and Environment)

One of the positive effects of music comes from its ability to remind us of previous memories and environments. Scientifically, it is tapping into our context-dependent memory. Let's say college was the happiest time of your life. If you start listening to the music that you were listening to at that time, it can help you feel more connected to that happier time in your life, and reminiscing about it can help reduce your stress.[80]

If you currently feel like you've hit a wall and can't move forward, sometimes you need to switch up your routine to get going again. One simple change you can make is to listen to different music. If you always listen to the same tunes during your commute or workout, you might be reinforcing your current negative mood or habits.[81] Try finding new music to help stimulate or calm your mind. Classical music in particular has been shown to relax the body and reduce blood pressure.[82]

Lighten your day (5 minutes):

Do you have a favorite song that can transport you to a time and place where you were happy? If so, take a five-minute break to listen to that song and take yourself away from your current stress. If you need to relax at the end of a stressful day, try putting on some classical music to help you decompress.

Emotional Freedom Technique®
(**LIGH**TEN™: **I**magination, **G**enius and **H**ealth)

The Emotional Freedom Technique (EFT) is a remarkable healing modality based on the same principles that have been used for thousands of years in acupuncture, but without the needles. When I was going through my divorce, EFT helped me calm down when my ex-wife triggered negative emotions.

While there are different variations, the basic "tapping" process is as follows:

1. Get in touch with the feeling related to the stressful situation you are dealing with.

2. Gently tap a part of your body as you say, "I feel (state your emotion) about (identify person or situation). I deeply and completely accept myself." Keep repeating this as you tap the following locations, in this exact order:

   a. outside of your hand

   b. between your eyebrows

   c. under eye

   d. under nose

   e. mid-chin

   f. collarbone

   g. under armpit

   h. top of head

3. Gently grasp your right wrist with your left hand and anchor into a feeling of gratitude by recalling a specific experience for which you are grateful for. Take a deep breath.[83]

When my therapist first demonstrated EFT to me, I thought it was hokey until I noticed its effectiveness. Don't judge the process just by what you read or see: give it a try and then decide if it works for you.

Lighten your day (5 minutes):

Next time you are feeling stressed, search for "Brad Yates Tapping" on YouTube.com and select any of his videos with a title that appeals to you. Follow along as he guides you through the tapping process and notice if your anxiety level has gone down once you complete the process.

Turn Your Dream into a Goal

(LIGHTEN™: Imagination, Genius, and Time)

We all have dreams, and not just the ones that we have during our sleep. We imagine ourselves traveling, having a loving relationship, a great job, a cool car, a home to call our own, financial freedom, and many more. Unfortunately, our dreams remain just a dream unless we turn the dream into a goal.

Goals are dreams with deadlines. The human mind won't move in the direction of a generality; it will move when it has something specific to aim at. Give your dream a deadline, and you will see movement. The more movement you experience, the more success you will have.[84] And as your dreams become reality, your stress becomes a thing of the past.

You can start with the big-picture dream with its deadline, and then work backwards by thinking of the small steps you can take to get you to your final destination.

For example, let's say you are dreaming about a new car. Write down the make, model, and color of the car you want, along with the month and year that you want to buy that car. Now list out the key things you need to do in order to reach your goal. It could be saving extra money per month for the down payment, doing online research on the options available, and taking the car for a test drive. Whatever those milestones are, put a deadline on each of these to keep your momentum. You might even consider asking a friend to check regularly on your progress to keep you moving forward.

To help solidify the description of your big picture goal (dream), consider structuring it as a SMART goal:[85]

- **Specific:** What exactly you want to accomplish.

- **Measurable:** How you will know when it is accomplished. What proof will you use?

- **Achievable:** How realistic your goal is given your resources. Make sure it is something you can control.

- **Relevant:** Why is it worth doing it at this time and the impact you expect.

- **Time-Bound:** What are the milestone deadlines for achieving your goal?

Lighten your day (5-10 minutes):

Do you frequently daydream about something that you really want but your inner critic tells you it's not possible? Write down your dream as something specific you want to achieve by a certain date.

Keep that written goal on your desk where you can see it.

List out the activities you need to complete to move forward and start taking small action steps towards reaching that goal. As you gain momentum you will be that much closer to turning your dream into a reality while building your confidence and reducing your stress along the way.

Forgive Your Past
(**L**I**GH**T**E**N™: **I**magination, **G**enius, **T**ime, and **N**etwork)

Do you feel guilty about something in the past? The burden of this past event is likely adding unnecessary stress that has been building for days, months, or years. It's time to forgive your past.

Forgiveness is giving up the hope that the past could have been any different. It's accepting the past for what it was and using the present moment to help yourself move forward. It is letting go so that the past does not hold you prisoner.[86]

👍 "I have lots of guilt about not being fully present as I was raising my son. Writing him letters helped me to forgive myself and to move forward."

—DORIS M., CLIENT

Lighten your day (10-30 minutes):

Write a letter to someone you feel guilt toward. Explain why you feel this way and ask them to forgive you. This can be written to someone dead or alive, or it can be written to yourself if it was related to self-sabotage. Whatever the case, the act of writing the letter will be therapeutic and help reduce the burden of stress you have been carrying from the past.

Play Relaxing Sounds
(**LIGHTEN**™: **I**magination, **G**enius, **T**ime, and **E**nvironment)

If listening to music proves too much of a distraction or you need something that you can listen to continuously to calm you throughout the day, consider playing relaxing sounds instead. If you own an Amazon Echo, you can say "Alexa, play me relaxing sounds" and it will cycle through nature sounds, such as ocean waves and birdsong.

You can also download an app called Relax Melodies (**https://www.ipnos.com/apps/relax-melodies/**) that allows you to customize over 50 nature noises and other soothing sounds that can be played simultaneously or individually. Playing calming sounds can help you maintain a more relaxed and less stressful presence during the day and can also help you fall asleep at night.

> **Lighten your day (30 minutes):**
>
> *Download the Relax Melodies app on your phone. Select two or three favorite sounds from nature and play them quietly or with headphones at your desk (to not disturb your coworkers) while you are working on a project. Notice if the soothing sounds help you minimize your stress level.*

Parts Integration

(**LIGHTEN**™: **L**ivelihood, **I**magination, **G**enius, **H**ealth, **T**ime, **E**nvironment, and **N**etwork)

Have you ever thought to yourself, "Part of me wants to do this and part of me doesn't"? Me too. This inner conflict, if left unresolved, will continue to fester inside of you as these unresolved emotions churn and create unnecessary stress in your life.

The solution to this dilemma is getting more understanding of those conflicts and working on uniting the divided parts under a common goal or intention. The process requires you to get in touch with your unconscious mind and visualize what each part's positive intention is for your common good. During the process, your disparate "parts" unite under a common purpose and the inner conflict dissipates as a result.

The process is extremely effective and provides near immediate stress relief as the conflict you were experiencing no longer exists. And it can work for just about any aspect of your life.

You can see video demonstrations and read more about the process by Googling "parts integration process nlp." Note that it is recommended to work with a trained professional to ensure the process works effectively for you.

> **Lighten your day (30-60 minutes):**
>
> *If you have a decision that has been lingering and causing you stress, it's best to work with a trained professional to get the most out of a parts-integration process rather than trying to do it yourself. Please contact me at **PeteAlexander.com** or reach out to AIPonline.org for a referral.*

Determine Your Personal Values

(**LIGHTEN**™: **L**ivelihood, **I**magination, **G**enius, **H**ealth, **T**ime, **E**nvironment, and **N**etwork)

I was first exposed to "personal values work" in the mid-1990s when I got certified in Managing Professional Growth (MPG®),[87] a program that is designed to align an employee's personal values with the key responsibilities of their professional role. The end result is an employee who is more productive, loyal, and engaged with their work.

At the time, I found that learning my own personal values was quite insightful. Specifically, I didn't list health as a high priority. Of course, later in life health became the number-one value for me, as it does with most everyone who experiences a life-altering medical crisis. And freedom (to do what I want) has become second only to health on my priority list as my career has progressed.

Your values are the things that you believe are important in the way you live and work. They should determine your priorities and, deep down, they're probably the measures you use to tell if your life is turning out the way you want it to.

Identifying and understanding your values is a challenging and important exercise. Your personal values are a central part of who you are—and who you want to be. By becoming more aware of these important factors in your life, you can use them as a guide to make the best choice in any situation. Some of life's decisions are really about determining what you value most. When many options seem reasonable, it's helpful and comforting to rely on your values and use them as a strong guiding force to pull you in the right direction.

To determine what your personal values are, follow these steps:[88]

1. Identify the times when you were happiest both professionally and personally. List what you were doing, who you were with, and other details about those events.

2. Identify the times when you were most proud both professionally and personally. Describe why you were proud, who you were with, and other details about those events.

3. Identify the times when you were most fulfilled and satisfied, either professionally or personally. Describe how and why this experience gave your life meaning, and other details about those events.

4. Determine your top values, based on your experiences of happiness, pride, and fulfillment. Ask yourself what was important to you in those experiences listed in questions 1-3. Just list them out in no particular order.

5. Prioritize your top-five values. Look at the first two values and ask yourself, "If I could satisfy only one of these, which would I choose?" For each value that ranks higher, compare it to the next value on your list. Keep ranking each value until you have an initial list, then double check the list starting at the bottom. Once you have double checked your list, you now have your list of top values.

The values that rank one to five on your list are your highest priority and should be used as reference whenever you are making an important decision, because only when you are in alignment with your personal values will that decision reduce your stress.

If you are having difficulty deciding on your personal values, consider working with a professional trained in values elicitation. Please contact me at **PeteAlexander.com** or reach out to **AIPonline.org** for a referral.

Lighten your day (1 hour):

Understanding your high-priority personal values helps you stay in alignment with what's important to you and reduces the stress around difficult decisions you have to make. To determine your personal values, follow the steps listed above, and refer to them when you have a challenging decision to make.

Unconsciously Ponder a Problem
(**LIGHTEN**™: **L**ivelihood, **I**magination, **G**enius, **T**ime, and **N**etwork)

If you feel like you are burning the midnight oil trying to solve a problem, take advantage of the power of your unconscious mind to do the processing and analysis for you. To do this, think of a problem that requires creative thought, and ask your unconscious mind to work on it overnight.

Alternatively, think about a big decision you need to make that your unconscious mind can help you with. Research has shown that when we switch off from consciously thinking about the problem, our unconscious mind takes over and is a very effective creative thinker and decision-maker.[89]

By delegating the work to your unconscious mind, your active mind can take a break and you will naturally feel less stress. In the morning, review what you wrote and see what your unconscious mind came up with while you were dreaming. You might surprise yourself.

Lighten your day (6-8 hours):

Have a challenging problem to solve or difficult decision to make? Do the following:

1. *Write the problem or decision down on a piece of paper or on your electronic device.*

2. *Read it out loud and ask your unconscious mind to take over from your active mind and work on it overnight.*

3. *In the morning, review what you wrote and see what your unconscious mind came up with.*

Mental and Emotional Release (MER)™

(**LIGHTEN**™: **L**ivelihood, **I**magination, **G**enius, **H**ealth, **T**ime, **E**nvironment, and **N**etwork)

I've saved the most complicated yet impactful tool for the end of this chapter. Many of us have stress that has been building for years (emotional baggage) that is out of proportion to the trigger that makes you react negatively in the first place. The only way to truly lead a less stressful life is to remove this baggage.

MER™ is a process that works with your unconscious and the memories that your unconscious has organized according to your individual "timeline." Using a specific interview process, a masterful MER practitioner helps you uncover the "root cause" of the baggage (which may or may not appear to be a significant event to your active mind). Then the master practitioner guides you back to the root cause, having you float over your timeline to retrieve the learning that you were supposed to gain from the experience and release the negative emotion.[90]

MER has been proven effective with addressing emotional baggage such as anger, fear, sadness, and guilt. (Incidentally, guilt is only good for pushing you toward making things right again. After that, it becomes shame, and shame is a toxic substance which will eat you up inside.)

MER is also effective in helping you remove your limiting beliefs, which are preventing you from moving forward with a challenge, expressed in statements such as, "I can't" or "it's too hard." If you are not sure if you have a limiting belief, there is a great worksheet that artist and speaker Phil Hansen created that can help you get clarity around this subject.[91]

Not only has MER worked for me, it has worked for many of my clients who get the breakthrough experience that comes from having their emotional baggage disappear. The only downside of this process is that some of my clients have a hard time believing that their baggage is indeed gone. That's because of our mistaken belief that we need years of therapy sessions when we just need to address the root cause of the negative emotions.

Negative emotions disappear using MER because they require time to express their meaning. Therefore, a switch in the temporal perspective (timeline) reframes the emotion. Switching the temporal perspective also shows the emotion to be the illusion it is, and it thus disappears in our unconscious mind.

Here's the caveat: you must be willing to trust the process and get in touch with your unconscious mind. I know it sounds sort of "woo-woo" in the short description above. I was a skeptic as well until I experienced it firsthand and felt a dramatic shift in my overall demeanor. I was so compelled by this technique that I committed to becoming a master practitioner of MER to help others get rid of their emotional baggage.

"I had a mind-blowing experience when I was extremely stressed at work and Professor Alexander was able to have an MER session with me over the phone. I realized that it all was triggered by my childhood experiences and throughout the break through session I was able to release that. He also taught me techniques that help me in my everyday life. Amazing!"

—OLGA S., CLIENT

Lighten your day (1 day):

If you want to learn more about MER™ and what it can do for you, reach out to me at PeteAlexander.com or get a referral to another master practitioner from the Association of Integrative Psychology at www.aiponline.org.

Reflection Point

Now that we are at the end of this chapter, which stress-relief tool did you like best? What was it about the tool you liked? Making notes to yourself below will help commit what you've learned to memory:

The stress-relief tool I like best:

I will use this tool specifically for:

The one that worked best for you should be bookmarked so you can easily refer to it in the future. You can also share it with your friends and family as a way of giving back to your community. There are also video-instruction stress-relief tools available for you to review and share by visiting my blog at **PeteAlexander.com**.

Earlier in this chapter, I described my client who was dealing with low self-worth. This issue did not just affect her professional life, it also manifested itself in her personal relationships and her physical health. She would let her parents and boyfriend walk all over her, she wasn't eating healthy, and she didn't want to exercise because she believed she wasn't beautiful. She was a train wreck at the young age of 28.

Fortunately, she was willing to do a breakthrough MER session where we addressed her low self-worth and other emotions that were keeping her stressed and stopping her becoming the person she wanted to be. After the MER process (which included identifying her personal values and conducting a parts-integration session), she overcame her limiting beliefs. She now has the confidence to communicate what she wants and expects from her employees and in her relationships. In addition, she is taking better physical care of herself, smiling more often, and looks years younger than when we first met.

Do you also want to look and feel younger than your actual age? You can by taking better care of your body. Check out the stress-relief tips in the next chapter on aligning your physical health.

Stress is nothing more than a socially acceptable
form of mental illness.

—RICHARD CARLSON, AMERICAN AUTHOR

CHAPTER 6

HEALTH—
Tips, Tools, and Techniques to
Relieve the Stress on Your Body

*When I look back on all these worries, I
remember the story of the old man who said on
his deathbed that he had had a lot of trouble in
his life, most of which had never happened.*

—Winston Churchill, former prime minister
of Great Britain

Early in my career, I had the opportunity to work for a management
consulting company that helped employees align their personal
values with the work they did. The theory was that employees
who aligned their ideals with their work were more productive, loyal,
and happy.

There were approximately 50 personal values in the program I worked
with, but google "personal values" and you'll find lists of many more. You
want to narrow your list down to the five values that are paramount to your
personal and professional success, similar to the values exercise discussed in
the previous chapter.

In most cases, those who participated in the values exercise forgot to list what I believe is the most important personal value we all should have: health. Why? Because we take our health for granted until we don't have it anymore, especially when we are young and foolish. And when we don't have our health, we don't want to do anything—work or pleasure—because it is too painful, or we don't have the energy to participate.

In 1974, my mother was diagnosed with malignant breast cancer and had to undergo a radical mastectomy of her left breast. She had contracted the cancer after a very stressful second divorce from my father (yes, they were married twice). After the surgery, her doctor gave her five years to live, which would have left me motherless as a teenager. Fortunately, the doctors were wrong, and my mother continues to defy modern medicine with the help of three techniques that I will detail later.

Appropriately, this chapter is dedicated to helping you with quick and easy actions for taking care of that one body you have been blessed with so that you can live a long and healthy life.

Remember: Each suggestion will have a key with the letter(s) highlighted in the word LIGHTEN™ to let you know that this tip, tool, or technique applies to that particular topic or topics of the model.

 = Author Uses Personally

 = Shortcut to Implementation

Deep Breathing

(**LIGHTEN**™: **L**ivelihood, **H**ealth, **T**ime, **E**nvironment, and **N**etwork)

When we get stressed and/or anxious, our breathing typically starts to escalate. By consciously slowing your breathing down, you tell your body that it is okay to calm down. It is also something you can practice whether you're in the office, car, on public transportation, or wherever.

A slight variation of this is a cooling (reverse) breath. You breath in through your mouth and out through your nose in slow deep breaths. You should feel a cooling, drying sensation over the top of your tongue. Air that comes in through your mouth is cooler because it's not warmed by the cilia in your nose. That cool sensation has a way of calming you.[92]

Just follow these steps with either standard deep breaths or cooling breaths, whichever you prefer:[93]

Lighten your day (1 minute):

1. *Sit on a chair with your spine straight. Relax your shoulders and try to release tension from your body.*

2. *Close your eyes and breathe normally for 30 seconds. During this time, try to relax your body even further.*

3. *Inhale deeply and exhale to the count of four. Pull your navel in as if you're trying to connect it with your spine.*

4. *If you have more than one minute to spare repeat the process for a few minutes more.*

Laughter

(LIGHTEN™: Imagination, Health, and Network)

You've probably heard the adage "laughter is the best medicine." In fact, science backs this up. Many studies have demonstrated the beneficial effects of laughter. Laughing elevates the pain threshold and can help break the cycle of pain, sleep loss, depression, and immunosuppression. Laughter lowers blood pressure and glucose levels, and increases glucose tolerance. Humor and laughter produce a discharge of endorphins with both euphoric and calming effects that provide stress relief.[94]

One of the great things about laughter is that it is contagious. Have you ever been in a room where other people are laughing hysterically, and you can't help yourself but smile and laugh also? Think about how good it feels to laugh out loud and, if you are lucky, laugh so hard that tears come out of your eyes.

Amazingly, you don't need a comedy film, a joke, or funny situation to use laughter to your advantage. Using the technique of Laughter Yoga, you simulate a deep hearty laughing session and still get the clinical benefits of laughing: a 28 percent drop in stress levels[95] even though there is nothing funny going on.

👍 "I got an unexpected tax bill and was worried about how I was going to find the money to pay for it. Then I saw Professor Alexander's blog post about this laughter technique and decided to give it a try. I couldn't believe how well it worked to calm my fears and help me get a clear head about how I was going to handle this bill."

—Debbie B., client

Lighten your day (1 minute):

1. *Imagine receiving a bill that's due or a report card that isn't complimentary. Pretend to open it in your hands and start laughing.*

2. *Imagine showing the bill or report card to others and keep laughing, the louder the better!*

3. *Breathe in deeply and notice how good it feels to laugh. Now you are ready to get back to your day.*

Proper Nutrition
(LIGHTEN™: **H**ealth)

Proper nutrition is a technique that goes under the "tell me something I don't know" category. So why am I including it? Because if I didn't, it would be an injustice. I'm not a health nut. I do enjoy occasional candy, ice cream, cake, and other pleasures. But a simple metaphor helped me reframe what I was putting in my body on a daily basis.

That metaphor is fuel. If you bought a new car, you wouldn't fill the gas tank with a sugary soft drink, would you? No, because you know that would damage your fuel system and lead to costly repairs. The same holds true for your body. If you fill your tank (stomach) regularly with sugary foods and drinks, your body will eventually break down and you will have costly repairs (in the form of medical bills).

Even if you are in great shape, it's a good idea to minimize or eliminate refined sugars, wheat products, and refined carbs. Those items can wreak havoc with your body by causing your blood sugar level to spike and crash—a one-two punch that can trigger a dramatic and sudden loss of energy and feelings of lethargy and exhaustion even with the best of us.[96]

Salt can be addictive, but research has shown that elevated levels of sodium blunt the body's natural responses to anxiety by inhibiting stress hormones that would otherwise be activated in challenging situations.[97] However, be mindful and check with your doctor first before using excessive salt to reduce your stress.

The best rule of thumb is moderation. Your body will thank you and you will have one less thing (your health) to worry about.

Lighten your day (1 minute):

Think of food as your body's fuel. Think twice at every meal about whether what you are eating can be considered optimal fuel for the health of your body.

Smiling & Sunglasses
(LIGHTEN™: **G**enius, **H**ealth, **E**nvironment, and **N**etwork)

When you see someone smiling, I bet you are wondering what they are smiling about because you want to smile too! Okay, not everyone wants to smile. I have encountered many curmudgeons who prefer to remain miserable, but most people I have interacted with enjoy smiling. I've tested this walking down the street thinking about something funny, with a smile on my face, and the majority of strangers I make eye contact with smile back.

When you frown, your brain thinks "Oh, I must not be feeling positive emotions." Whereas when it notices you flexing those muscles upward on the side of the mouth it thinks, "I must be smiling. Oh, we must be happy." And you don't even have to be happy to get the benefit. Just hold a smile for 60 seconds and notice yourself feeling better.

You know what is even more amazing? Research shows smiling gives the brain as much pleasure as 2,000 bars of chocolate, or $25,000.[98] Now, that's a lot of chocolate and a lot of money.

And if you find yourself smiling outdoors in the daylight, maximize the benefits of smiling by putting on sunglasses. When you squint, that tells your brain that you are worried. So, smiling and sunglasses make for a powerful stress relief combination.

 "I'm well on my way to making $25,000 worth of smiles now. Hopefully, the Feds don't find out or they will want to tax me."

—BOB S., CLIENT

Lighten your day (1 minute):

As you are walking to or from your car, force yourself to smile and hold it for at least 60 seconds. Try to make eye contact with at least one other person while you are smiling. Do you feel any different? If it is a sunny day, don't forget to wear your sunglasses to maximize the benefits from your smiling efforts!

Keep Your Head Up
(**LIGH**TEN™: **I**magination, **G**enius, and **H**ealth)

Have you ever noticed when you are down that you tend to hold your head down too? It's your body's natural reaction to your negative thoughts. When you think about things, notice whether your head is up (positive—thinking about future) or down (negative—thinking about the past). Make a conscious effort to keep your head up as you are contemplating your current situation.

> **Lighten your day (1 minute):**
>
> *Make a conscious effort to keep your head up, even for a minute. Focus on something at eye level or higher. Notice how this simple movement can make a positive difference in your overall mood.*

Traction
(LIGHTEN™: **H**ealth)

When you are stressed, chances are your back and shoulders tighten up. I used to suffer from chronic lower back pain. It would flare up under stressful conditions, and there were times when I couldn't be comfortable no matter if a stood or sat. I spent a lot of time and money with chiropractors who would provide only temporary relief.

Then I learned how to use a simple pull-up bar that you can attach to a doorframe. When your back and shoulders are tight, you hang on this bar for 30-60 seconds and the pull of your weight on your muscles and joints (traction) opens up your vertebrae and stretches your shoulders. Do this once or twice a day and you may be able to say goodbye to the chiropractor. Just search for "pull-up bar" on **amazon.com** and pick one that fits your preferences and budget.

 "I started using a pull-up bar to stretch my lower back when it got stiff. Now I use it to stretch my whole body and de-stress after a long day at work."

—IGOR T., CLIENT

Lighten your day (1 minute):

Go to a playground or gym and find a stable horizontal bar that is at least a few inches taller than you. Hold the bar with both hands, and then flex your knees so that the weight of your body transfers from your legs to your arms. Hang there for 30-60 seconds, letting your back and shoulders stretch. Bring your legs back straight and release the bar. Do your back and/or shoulders feel better? If so, do this daily to relieve tension that builds up in your body. Having your own pull-up bar at home makes it even more convenient to make it a daily habit.

Temple Touch
(LIGHTEN™: Health)

You know when you start to get that achy feeling that a headache is on its way? Or you already have a headache but neither coffee nor aspirin is doing the trick?

One of my favorite self-care tips is to apply pressure with your hands at the center of your forehead and then press firmly down as you slide your fingers horizontally apart, ending at your temples. Keep your eyes closed while you do this and repeat ten times. This process should relax your tension and provide you with stress relief.

> **Lighten your day (1 minute):**
>
> Sit back in your chair. Close your eyes. Put your three middle fingers of each hand in the center of your forehead, apply pressure, and move them horizontally towards your temples. Repeat ten times and notice the calming effect this process provides.

Avoid Intoxication

(**LIGH**TEN™: **I**magination, **G**enius, and **H**ealth)

I grew up in a highly dysfunctional family who considered alcohol one of the five food groups. Members of my family would numb themselves with alcohol in good times and bad, and the bad times would get worse because they couldn't handle the intoxication.

Rather than forgetting your failures by numbing the pain with alcohol, it is far more effective to etch your failures into your brain so that you can ensure you learn from them. When you turn to the bottle every time things don't go your way, you will not give your brain a clear opportunity to learn from that experience. And as an additional bonus, not intoxicating yourself can improve your health, sleeping cycles, focus, willpower and your bank account.[99]

> **Lighten your day (1 minute):**
>
> Don't use drugs or alcohol when things are not going your way. Instead, honestly ask yourself what life learning you are getting from the experience of failure. This will give your brain the opportunity to absorb this learning into your unconscious, making you stronger, more resilient, and less stressed in the future.

Shake It Off

(LIGHTEN™: Livelihood, Imagination, Health, Environment, and Network)

In some African cultures, shaking therapy is used for emotional healing. The literal shaking symbolically wards off perceived emotional threat of fear, self-doubt, or worry. By doing a quick body shake, you can release the emotional attachments causing tension as you get blood flowing rapidly through your body.

As a bonus, you might end up laughing as you shake, boosting your mood and further reducing your stress.

Lighten your day (1 minute):

Find a private area (even a bathroom stall if you don't have a conference room or office you can go into) and channel your favorite music performer, or do your best dance move, or mimic a wet dog coming out of the water. Start to shake, twist, or whatever you can do to get your whole body moving for about 30 seconds. Take a deep breath and go on with your day.

Scream into a Pillow

(LIGHTEN™: Health and Environment)

It works. It really works. Just like singing and laughing, screaming increases blood flow and oxygen to help your body fend off stress. Best of all, your pillow won't scream back.

Lighten your day (1 minute):

When you are home and feeling particularly stressed, grab a large bed pillow, sit or lie down, and scream into it as loud as you can. Take a few deep breaths and repeat as necessary until you feel the tension removed from your body.

Dark Chocolate

(LIGHTEN™: **H**ealth)

More research needs to be done, but recent studies suggest several possible health benefits of dark chocolate and cocoa, including helping people with chronic fatigue syndrome. Researchers believe that chocolate enhances the action of neurotransmitters, like serotonin, which help regulate mood and sleep.[100] And when you regulate your mood and sleep, you tend to be less stressed.

> *All you need is love. But a little chocolate now and then doesn't hurt.*

—CHARLES M. SCHULTZ, AMERICAN CARTOONIST

Lighten your day (1 minute):

Keep a bar of dark chocolate in your desk to pull out in a stressful emergency. Just remember to eat it in moderation.

Chew Gum

(LIGHTEN™: Livelihood, Health, and Network)

I've never been a fan of someone chewing gum at work, especially if they are chewing with their mouth wide open. There is something about hearing the crackling of the gum and spit that makes me want to put my headphones on. Maybe it's because my ex-wife chewed gum loudly every time we met during our divorce proceedings. Hmmm…

Nevertheless, chewing gum has been clinically shown to help with stress relief in some instances. Study participants who chewed gum showed significantly better alertness and reduced state anxiety, stress, and salivary cortisol, which is your body's main stress hormone that works with your brain to help your mood.[101]

Lighten your day (1 minute):

Keep a pack of your favorite flavor of sugar-free gum in your desk for the next time you feel stressed. Just be mindful to chew your gum quietly so that it doesn't disturb your coworkers.

Clench Your Bottom

(LIGHTEN™: Livelihood and Health)

Yes, you read that right! I didn't just put this one in just to see if you were paying attention. This technique truly exists, and there is a full book that was written about this subject.[102]

The funny thing is that it seems to work for me. I incorporate it into my daily stretching routine, and I find that focusing on this activity in addition to my exercising actually provides a greater level of stress relief than stretching alone. The author says you can constrict your anus discreetly at any time … while commuting, in a meeting, or wherever convenient. Just remember to do it 100 times in one session.

This technique reminds me of several jokes I have incorporated into my presentations, depending on my audience. One of them is the following: *What did the proctologist say when he went to write a prescription and pulled out a rectal thermometer?* "Some a★★hole walked off with my pen!" If we ever get to meet in person, remind me to tell you some others. They are pretty funny, just like this technique.

Lighten your day (1-2 minutes):

During a meeting, try constricting your anus 100 times. If nothing else, it will help you focus and, at best, it will decrease your stress.

Take Care of Your Skin
(LIGHTEN™: **G**enius, **H**ealth, and **T**ime)

Have you ever noticed that your skin breaks out more when you're stressed? Anxiety causes a chemical response that makes your skin more sensitive. Your body also produces more cortisol when stressed, which causes your sebaceous glands to produce more oil. More oil means oily skin that is prone to acne.

Taking an extra few minutes before you go to bed to wash your face and remove any facial products and makeup you've worn during the day will make a world of difference. If you're prone to oily or dry skin, choose skin care products that are specifically designed for your skin type.[103]

It's important not to neglect your skin-care routine, especially when you're stressed and tired. Your skin will thank you for it.

Lighten your day (1-5 minutes):

Your body reacts to your stress, and your skin is your billboard to the outside world. Take a few minutes each night or morning to clean and care for your skin, and you won't advertise acne or other blemishes to others.

Singing

(**LIGHTE**N™: **I**magination, **H**ealth, **T**ime, and **E**nvironment)

Do you have a favorite song? Similar to laughing, singing is a great remedy for anxiety because it increases blood flow and oxygen, which helps to release stress and restore balance. Great places to sing your favorite tunes include the shower and in the car. You can use your creativity and imagine yourself on stage performing to an adoring audience, and you won't have to worry about stage fright!

Lighten your day (1-5 minutes):

Stuck in traffic? Put your favorite song on your stereo and sing to your heart's content. Don't worry about other drivers seeing you—just imagine they are your adoring audience. Not only will this help you pass the time, it will reduce your stress level as well.

Be Mindful of Food on Business Trips

(**LIGHTEN**™: **L**ivelihood, **I**magination, **H**ealth, and **E**nvironment)

One of the perks I enjoy when I travel is the variety of food options in the various cities I visit. However, that used to come with an unexpected cost that I couldn't expense to my company. I noticed that my waistline had often expanded by the time I got back from any trip that lasted more than a couple days. I realized that I had to be mindful of what I was eating while on business, especially after my ER/intensive care unit visit, and I suggest you do the same to limit unnecessary stress on your body.

First, you simply need to be aware that business travel can predispose you to making poorer nutritional decisions. The steak with fries and a late-night cocktail at the hotel bar might seem justifiable as a reward for acing a long day of client meetings. But research finds that restaurant food contains more calories per serving, is higher in total fat and saturated fat per calorie and contains less dietary fiber than meals prepared at home. Research also suggests that the higher calorie content of restaurant food is compounded by chronic stress, like that caused by frequent business travel, which is linked to preferences for even more high-calorie foods.[104]

A great way to be mindful of this is to carry a copy of the restaurant edition of *Eat This Not That!*[105] that can help you make meal decisions when it isn't obvious what the right choice is from the menu. If you think twice about having that late evening heavy meal, your body will appreciate it.

Lighten your day (1-5 minutes):

A healthier and less-stressed body starts with the fuel we put into it. When you are on a business trip, take along a copy of the restaurant edition of Eat This Not That! and review some of the entries you have ordered in the past. Choose other options on the menu that are healthier but still tasty enough that they don't make you feel like you are on a diet.

Have More Sex
(LIGHTEN™: **H**ealth and **N**etwork)

I categorize this one in the "no-duh" category, too. Yes, of course, having more sex will help you relax, help you sleep better, and connect with your partner, which all leads to less stress in your life overall.[106] Enough said.

It does remind me of one of my favorite jokes, however. Do you know what sex and pizza have in common? When they're good, they're really good. But when they're bad, they're still pretty good.

Lighten your day (at least 3 minutes):

Have more sex. No more explanation necessary.

Roll Out Your Stress
(LIGHTEN™: **H**ealth and **E**nvironment)

Muscles tight in your shoulders, lower back or legs? A simple self-care technique for stress relief is to use a foam roller while lying on the floor. It allows you to effectively massage areas of your body quickly without the added time and cost of a real massage. It's especially effective after dealing with a stressful commute or holiday shopping.[107]

And if you are short on cash and don't have the money to buy a foam roller, an old tennis ball might also do the trick.

Lighten your day (5-10 minutes):

Google "foam rollers" and order one that fits your budget. Choose one that is advertised as on the softer side, to be more forgiving on your muscles. Take a few minutes in the evening to roll out your tight muscles while watching your favorite show or listening to music.

Exercise

(LIGH**TEN**™: **H**ealth)

I'm not going to waste your time by telling you that exercise is good for you. However, what you might not realize is that exercise in almost any form can act as a stress reliever. According to the Mayo Clinic, being active can boost your feel-good endorphins and distract you from daily worries.[108] I know this because hiking and cycling did wonders for my mood when I was going through my divorce. So did stretching my back and shoulders when I got home from work.

It doesn't take a lot. Go for a short walk at lunch. Take the stairs instead of the elevator. Every little bit helps.

Lighten your day (10 minutes):

Take the stairs instead of the elevator/ escalator and/or take a 10-minute walk at lunch. Whatever it is, just move more if you are generally sedentary during the day. Your body and mind will thank you.

Shower for Body AND Mind

(LIGHTEN™: Imagination and Health)

You already know that you should shower regularly for personal hygiene, but showers can also be a great way to help you relax. If you work at home, try taking a "just for the heck of it" shower at lunch time, or if you have a gym near your work, just take a shower even if you didn't work out and you are not sweaty. Showers work wonders to refresh your mood and relieve your stress.

Lighten your day (10 minutes):

Take a quick shower just for the heck of it. Not first thing in the morning as you are rushing to work or some other activity; rather, take it when you can feel your stress building. This 10-minute diversion will help you refresh.

Drink More Water

(LIGHTEN™: Health)

Considering that our bodies are mostly water, you need to be aware of the vital importance of hydration. Not everyone realizes that the health benefits of hydration extend to stress relief. Being even just a little dehydrated can increase our body's levels of cortisol, the stress hormone, leading to feelings of anxiety, exhaustion, and overall irritability.[109]

To avoid getting dehydrated, calculate how much water your body needs at rest. That's working at a desk, puttering around the house, reading, and doing all of the other things you do throughout the day. This is your bare minimum water requirement for what your body needs to function.

The simple equation for determining this is to divide your body weight in two and drink half your body weight in ounces (not literally half your weight). So, if you weigh 200 pounds, you would need 100 ounces of water per day if you're not doing anything strenuous. If you're working out or hiking at a high altitude or outdoors, you're going to need to add to those 100 ounces.[110]

When I first found out about this equation, I had a very hard time drinking that much. However, I soon noticed that I felt better, and I started losing weight as I drank more and more water. The downside of course were more frequent stops at the bathroom, but that was an excuse for me to get up and move around during the day. I also found that adding a little Stevia natural sweetener helped make drinking water much easier for me, especially when I discovered different Stevia flavors from **SweetLeaf.com**.

Lighten your day (10 minutes):

Figure out how many ounces of water per day you should be drinking using the simple equation above. Get a water bottle that has the ounces marked on the outside. Experiment with different natural sweeteners to flavor your water. Commit to drinking the recommended amount of water for your body to get the health benefits.

Take a Power Nap

(**LIGHTEN**™: **L**ivelihood, **I**magination, **G**enius, **H**ealth, **T**ime, **E**nvironment, and **N**etwork)

One of the ideas discussed in this chapter is the importance of getting good sleep. Well, when shit happens, we sometimes cannot get the recommended seven to nine hours of sleep per night. On those occasions, taking a power nap might help with your stress level.

A clinical study found that people who stay awake throughout the day become progressively more sensitive to negative emotions. In contrast, those who take an afternoon nap are desensitized to negative emotions yet more responsive to positive ones.[111] No wonder many high-tech companies offer sleeping pods and quiet rooms for their employees.

While the study gave participants the opportunity for 90 minutes of sleep, most sleep experts agree that if you want to have a quick jolt of alertness, vigor, and/or decrease fatigue, take a 10- to 20-minute nap.[112]

Lighten your day (20-30 minutes):

Are you dozing off at work in the afternoon? Rather than potentially making mistakes that will bring you stress later, do the following: find a quiet room. Set your alarm timer for 20 minutes, sit or lie down and close your eyes. Breathe deeply in and out until you fall asleep. When the alarm sounds, give yourself another minute or two to fully wake up before returning to your work.

Grounding Through Earthing
(**LIGH**TEN™: **I**magination, **G**enius, **H**ealth, and **E**nvironment)

Scientific research indicates that your body can be protected and helped when you electrically reconnect to the Earth. That is, when you are grounded. These studies have indicated that grounding helps to decrease our levels of inflammation, improve circulation, and reduce our stress levels.[113] But with all the electronics in our daily life, we have a tendency to lose our electrical connection. And wearing shoes doesn't help.

Walking barefoot in conductive surfaces such as grass, dirt, sand, or even concrete is all it takes to draw the earth's energy. Note that wood, asphalt, and vinyl are not conductive. And if you don't have the time or desire to go outside barefoot, there are alternative products you can purchase for your home such as pads for your bed, floor, or favorite chair. Simply Google "earthing mat" to learn more.

 "I have been dealing with a lot of stress due to my job and the difficult organization I work for. I was getting physical ailments such as stomach aches, and I couldn't sleep very well. Professor Alexander suggested I go to my favorite beach and connect with the sand and ocean. I can't believe what a difference that made in my energy! After walking barefoot on the beach for only a half hour, I went from being lethargic to full of life! I'm going to be making frequent visits to the beach now."

—SUNSHINE T., CLIENT

Lighten your day (30 minutes):

Find a patch of grass, dirt, or sand to be barefoot on. This could be your backyard, a park, or beach. You can stand, walk, or sit, just ensure your bare feet are in contact with the earth. Feel the energy of the earth through your feet and notice how much more relaxed you become.

Trauma Release Exercises
(LIGHTEN™: Imagination, Genius, and Health)

We've discussed previously about how our body carries stress in our neck, shoulders, back, and joints. These are the obvious signs and signals our body is giving us. However, if you have been carrying significant anxiety and emotional baggage inside you for years, this next tool could benefit you.

Trauma Release Exercises (TRE®) is an innovative program that assists the body in releasing deep muscular patterns of stress, tension, and trauma. The exercises safely activate a natural reflex mechanism of shaking or vibrating that releases muscular tension, calming down the nervous system. When this muscular shaking/vibrating mechanism is activated in a safe and controlled environment, the body is encouraged to return to a state of balance. TRE is based on the fundamental idea—backed by research—that stress, tension, and trauma are psychological and physical. TRE's reflexive muscle vibrations generally feel pleasant and soothing. After doing TRE, many people report feelings of peace and well-being.[114]

If you are interested in this technique, you can buy a book[115] or video[116] to help walk you through the process. However, it might be best to first start by attending a workshop[117] facilitated by a trained professional to see if this process works for you.

I first experienced TRE at a weekend retreat, and while it was quite strenuous on my body, I felt an enormous amount of stress relief, which convinced me of its merits.

Lighten your day (30 minutes):

Review the information on TraumaPrevention.com and sign up for a workshop to see if you can benefit from TRE®.

Get a Massage
(LIGHTEN™: **H**ealth and **E**nvironment)

As stress builds, we tend to carry it in our neck, shoulders, and lower back. Over time, this body tension can affect our productivity and our quality of life. Treating yourself to a professional massage could be just the ticket to help you cope. In an hour or less, you can get a full body massage, or treat a particular area of your body. You come out of the massage feeling refreshed and relaxed.

If it is inconvenient to schedule, or you are uncomfortable with the idea of going to a spa and having a stranger massage you, consider getting a massage chair for your home. There are several stores where you can give them a try (in airports, for example) to see what features might be of interest to you. I bought a massage chair for my home, and I find that using it for just 15 minutes in the evening before I go to bed helps me relax and get to sleep quicker. The money I have saved versus spa massages has more than paid for the chair.

Lighten your day (1 hour):

Muscles stiff from all your stress? Treat yourself to a massage or invest in a massage chair to relax in the comfort of your own home.

Get Good Quality Sleep
(**LIGHTEN**™: **L**ivelihood, **I**magination, **G**enius, **H**ealth, **T**ime, **E**nvironment, and **N**etwork)

I know, this is another one of those obvious tools. And if you are extremely busy, like most of us, you probably stress about getting good sleep—there's an irony for you.

There are some very simple ways you can ensure a better night's sleep, even if work and/or some other issue(s) are giving you anxiety. For example, give these a try:

- No electronics in the bedroom. No TV, no phone, no laptop, no nothing unless it is a simple alarm clock. The phone is the biggest perpetrator, as a simple text or ping is like Pavlov's dog responding to a stimulus. Once that ping wakes our brain up, we have a harder time getting back to sleep.

- Go to bed at the same time each night, and follow a consistent ritual (brushing your teeth, putting sleeping clothes on, etc.) teaching your body and mind to expect sleep.

- Use the bed for only two things: rest and sex. If you work at home, don't work while lying in bed because it will confuse your body and make it harder for you to fall asleep when you really want to.

The key determinants of quality sleep include:[118]

- Falling asleep in 30 minutes or less
- Waking up no more than once per night; and
- Being awake for 20 minutes or less after initially falling asleep.

And one of the big mistakes we can make is to try and catch up on our sleep on the weekends. Though it feels good temporarily, having an inconsistent wake-up time disturbs your natural sleep pattern. Your body cycles through an elaborate series of sleep phases in order for you to wake up rested and refreshed. One of these phases involves preparing your mind to be awake and alert, which is why people often wake up just before their alarm clock goes off (the brain is trained and ready).

When you sleep past your regular wake-up time on the weekend, you end up feeling groggy and tired. This isn't just disruptive to your day off, it also makes you less productive on Monday because your brain isn't ready to wake up at your regular time. If you need to catch up on sleep, just go to bed earlier.[119]

Lighten your day (8 hours):

Remove all electronics from your bedroom, except a simple alarm clock if you need an alarm to get you up in the morning. Go to bed at the same time each night and get up at the same time in the morning. Only use your bed for sleep and sex: no working or internet surfing.

Reflection Point

Now that we are at the end of this chapter, which stress-relief tool did you like best? What was it about the tool you liked? Making notes to yourself below will help commit what you've learned to memory:

The stress-relief tool I like best:

I will use this tool specifically for:

The one that worked best for you should be bookmarked so you can easily refer to it in the future. You can also share it with your friends and family as a way of giving back to your community. There are also video-instruction stress-relief tools available for you to review and share by visiting my blog at **PeteAlexander.com**.

If you are curious about the three stress-relief tools I mentioned earlier that my mother has used to defy modern medicine and live a long life, they all are included in this chapter. The first one is laughter. My mother has made it a daily habit to laugh, and her laugh is contagious. She doesn't hold back, and you can't help but to laugh with her.

The second is getting a good night's sleep. My mother is one of those lucky people who sleeps deeply based on the decibel level of her snoring (sorry, Mom!).

Third, chocolate has been one of my mother's five food groups since I was a toddler. The other four food groups include cookies, ice cream, milk, and candy. Note that my Mom did tell me that she would have eaten better when she was younger if she knew she would live so long, but she won't change anything now.

If you don't have time to laugh, get good sleep and/or enjoy a good piece of chocolate, then the next chapter and associated stress-relief tools will be of benefit to you.

Keep going on hikes, keep having your friends in your life, keep that downtime sacred as well because as hard as you work in any job, it's really nice to have the relaxing de-stressors. Stress is the worst thing. That's the ultimate demise of any good thing.

—DIANNA AGRON, AMERICAN ACTRESS

CHAPTER 7

TIME—
Tips, Tools, and Techniques
to Save Time so That You Can
Stress Less

*Time is free, but it's priceless. You can't own it,
but you can use it. You can't keep it, but you
can spend it. Once you've lost it, you can never
get it back.*

—HARVEY MACKAY, AMERICAN BUSINESSMAN AND AUTHOR

Time is our most precious resource, and once used, it is gone
forever. Our hectic lives demand more and more from us, but
there are still only 24 hours in the day. Since we cannot add
hours to the clock, we often find ourselves working late, working on
weekends, skipping exercise, and sleep just to try and keep up with all of
our responsibilities.

As children, we are scheduled in school. When we start our careers, it's
eight to five, Monday through Friday, and our calendars reign supreme. I
learned this the hard way during my first professional sales job as a FedEx
account executive.

I had a 7:00 a.m. sales call one Monday morning. Normally I would start work at 8:00 a.m., so that was early for me. As I got to my car, I opened my full-size 8.5"x11" day planner (remember those?) to find the address of where I was going. When I got to the customer site, about 15 minutes early, like I usually did, I reached for my planner, which had all my presentation materials as well. It wasn't there … and it wasn't anywhere inside my car.

Oh shit! I thought as my stomach dropped. I relied on that calendar for nearly everything I did for my job: my appointments, my contacts, my sales materials, you name it. And then I realized that in my grogginess, I had left my planner wide open on the roof of my car as I drove to the customer site. With my anxiety level way high, I wished at that point that I could go back in time. Since I couldn't, you'll just have to read to the end of this chapter to find out how I handled that stressful situation.

What if we could gain back time? No, I'm not talking about the daylight savings "fall back" when we get an extra hour of sleep. I'm talking about tips, tools, and techniques that can help you manage your time better so that you stress less and live more. Sound interesting? Then please read on.

Remember: Each suggestion will have a key with the letter(s) highlighted in the word LIGHTEN™ to let you know that this tip, tool, or technique applies to that particular topic or topics of the model.

 = Author Uses Personally

 = Shortcut to Implementation

Set Boundaries

(LIGHTEN™: Livelihood, Time, and Network)

It's happened to us all at one time or another. We say "yes" to every request to look like the good employee, friend, volunteer, etc., and then we stress over how we don't have time to do all the things we committed to. This is especially true when it comes to requests from the person we report to at work.

Years ago, I coauthored a book that provided tips and strategies to help organizations recruit and retain technical professionals. What we found was that no matter what perks the organization offered their employees, the number-one reason people left was their relationship with their manager.[120]

It's easy to blame our boss, employer, clients, or customers for our work-life balance getting out of whack, but it's not their fault. The reality is: no matter how demanding others are or how excessive their expectations may be, we're in charge of our own lives. We choose what to accept. If we're overworked by our employer, it's often because we've allowed it to get to that point; we didn't set proper boundaries.[121]

The simple solution is to learn how to say "no" to requests on your time. If you find this difficult, remind yourself that saying "no" allows you to say "yes" to the things that you truly want to do or really need to do.

> *Lighten your day (1 minute):*
>
> *Think about a time when a request was made of you that caused you stress. Replay that event in the following way: pause before answering the request and compare it to what you already have on your plate. If it is not as important and/or is something you do not want to do, kindly decline the request. If an explanation is necessary, mention that their request will delay other activities on your list of responsibilities. If it is your supervisor who has made the request, ask that person to select something else from your list of responsibilities that can be delayed if you attend to this request.*
>
> *Now that you have practiced setting boundaries, try it for real next time a request is made of you that causes you anxiety.*

Realize Work Expands
(**LIG**HTEN™: **L**ivelihood, **I**magination, **G**enius, and **T**ime)

If you are a workaholic by nature, there is a reality you need to face: you'll never get ALL your work done. There's no finish line. You can always find new work to do if you look for it. This means your decision to stop working can't be tied to your completion of responsibilities. Instead, you must learn to accept the inevitable, which is that there will always be undone tasks left on the table whenever you stop working.

When you realize you won't ever get everything done, you lessen the guilt associated with working less and become more comfortable with stepping away from it. You no longer judge your progress against an impossible goal.

This was an important realization for me, and hopefully it will be for you too.

Lighten your day (1 minute):

Set an alarm for the end of your workday. Commit to stopping what you are doing, turn off your occupational email on your phone, and go out for a nice dinner or stay home and curl up in front of the TV or with a good book. Resist looking at your email until the beginning of the next workday and pick up where you left off the previous day. Chances are you will be more refreshed, energetic, and less stressed during your day.

Understand Busy Does Not Equal Success
(**LI**GHTEN™: **L**ivelihood, **I**magination, and **T**ime)

"I'm busy." It's the common answer to the question of "how's it going?" You rarely, if ever, hear somebody reply, "Work is easy, and I'm on top of everything." This may seem like a minor conversational quirk, but it's reflective of a much larger issue. As long as we connect the idea that being busy equals being important and successful, we'll look for ways to keep making ourselves busier.

People brag about pulling an all-nighter to finish a project because they have no time. They eagerly share that they didn't have five minutes to think during the course of their busy day. And they describe eating lunch at their desk while simultaneously replying to emails and being on a conference call, as if they just mastered a new magic trick. Our success isn't tied to how busy we are, it's tied to how much control we have of our time and how we choose to use it.

Think about that last sentence for a moment. If we stop worrying about what other people are thinking about the hours we work and how much is on our plate, we can refocus our efforts on using our time as effectively as possible. Inevitably, we will have more time for meaningful ventures, and our stress will reduce as a result.

The reality is that being fully invested in "busy" is a long day's journey to nowhere. If all your efforts and time are used up being busy, then they are not being used to be clear, focused, and productive.[122]

Lighten your day (1 minute):

Start keeping a list to be more mindful of what is keeping you busy. Weed out activities that are not adding value to your career and/or home life.

Slow Down
(LIGHTEN™: **T**ime, **E**nvironment, and **N**etwork)

In the evening or on the weekends, do you find yourself rushing to get your chores done just to get them out of the way? Rather than adding stress to your life as another thing on your to-do list, your routine tasks could be more enjoyable.

How? By changing the way we think about the activity as something to be completed or hurried through to get to the next thing and, instead, considering the additional value that can come from doing the chore. For example, washing the dishes can become quality time with a loved one, and taking the trash out can become an opportunity to look at the stars.

When you slow down, you honor yourself and the present moment. You'll have more fun in your life, too, and this helps you handle stress more positively and easily.[123]

"My husband and I love doing dishes together. We laugh, and sometimes we even dance. Not only does this daily chore go faster, it brings us closer together."

—EMILY R., CLIENT

Lighten your day (1 minute):

Identify a mundane chore you typically rush through and think of a way that you can slow down and enjoy that time more. For example, you might add your favorite music or use that time to call somebody you haven't talked to in a while. This way the time you spend will feel more like quality, not quantity, thus reducing any stress associated with the chore.

One-Minute Rule
(**LIGHTEN**™: **L**ivelihood, **T**ime, and **E**nvironment)

Ever notice how chores or work piles up to the point where it feels overwhelming to even get started? Procrastination is often a vicious cycle because you delay and then you have less time to complete the project, so you get anxious, procrastinate more, have even less time, which makes you even more stressed.

Well, the one-minute rule could be your answer. Pick a single task that takes one minute or less to complete. For example:[124]

- Hang up a coat
- Read a letter and toss it

- Fill in a form

- Answer an email

- Jot down a citation

- Pick up phone messages

- File a paper

- Put a dish in the dishwasher

Completing just a single simple task can build positive momentum and help give you the confidence and energy to work on other tasks.

Lighten your day (1 minute):

Do any task if it only (truly) takes a minute. It reduces the stress associated with being overwhelmed by giving you a sense of accomplishment and progress.

Minimize Unproductive Meetings
(LIGHTEN™: Livelihood, Time, and Network)

Work-related meetings have increased in length and frequency over the past 50 years, to the point where executives spend an average of nearly 23 hours a week in them. And that doesn't even include all the impromptu gatherings that don't make it onto the schedule. Middle managers are also being burdened by unproductive meetings, keeping them from completing their own work while sacrificing deep thinking.[125]

Since time is a commodity we cannot get back, each hour we waste in an unproductive meeting means an hour lost to more productive work, and your stress level will increase as you inch closer to a project deadline. The more control you have of your time, the less anxious you feel.

A great way to help gain back some time in your schedule is to ask the organizer what role you have in the meeting, and truly determine if you need to participate. Sometimes you will get a response that they were just including you for your feedback, and you can easily decline to attend by asking them to send you what they need feedback on. Be especially wary of meetings without an agenda: that's a clear indicator that the organizer hasn't given the meeting much thought and you will likely suffer because of it.

I have found that standing-only meetings work great if you only want a meeting that lasts 15 minutes because people get right to the point. Another option is to be mindful of how many people are invited to the meeting. The more attendees in the meeting, the less productive they tend to be.

Lighten your day (1 minute):

Each time you receive a meeting invite and suspect it will be an unproductive use of your time, ask the organizer what role you have in the meeting and whether your participation is crucial. If it isn't, decline the meeting invitation and gain back that time in your schedule. The more control you have of your time, the less stressed you will feel.

Plan Your Day
(**LIGHTEN**™: **L**ivelihood, **I**magination, **T**ime, and **N**etwork)

As discussed previously, when we feel like we are not in control, our stress level increases. Therefore, it makes sense that the more we feel in control of our day, the less anxious we will feel, and research backs this up.

You can combat stress before it even starts by proactively planning your day, your week, and even your year so that you have more control of your time. Interestingly, and by no means a surprise, nearly 25 percent of our happiness is related to our ability to manage stress.[126]

Try planning today by the relationships that are most important to you, instead of by schedules or deadlines. Everything we do is really just a reflection of the relationships we have with others or with ourselves.[127] If you reflect this accordingly in your calendar (including "me time") you will be true to yourself and less anxious because of it.

Lighten your day (5 minutes):

On your daily calendar, block out chunks of time when your coworkers cannot schedule meetings so that you can work undisturbed. By planning your day to complete certain tasks in those blocks of time, you will be more productive, gain more control of your day, and feel less stressed.

Pack Your Bag the Night Before
(**LIGHTEN**™: **L**ivelihood and **T**ime)

Have you ever got to work, school or some other event and realized you forgot something that wasn't in your bag? It's happened to all of us. The rush to get to work or school or wherever in the morning makes it difficult to concentrate.

A simple technique that can save you a lot of stress in the morning is packing your bag the night before. Take five minutes before you go to bed to do this and you'll be less likely to forget something important like your schoolbook, wallet, office badge, or phone.[128] When you have everything you need for your day, you advert unnecessary stress.

Lighten your day (5 minutes):

Pack your bag for the next day before you go to bed. You will be less likely to forget something important that may cause you unnecessary stress during your day.

Arrive Early to Meetings
(**LI**GHTEN™: **L**ivelihood, **T**ime, and **N**etwork)

Have you ever noticed that when you are running late, everything starts slowing you down? You are running late for work and you hit all the red lights. You are running late for a meeting and your boss needs an immediate five-minute chat. That before-lunch meeting is running late, and now you don't have time to eat a proper meal. You get to the doctor's office late, and now you have to wait longer because the next person has already been admitted. And with every one of these occurrences, your stress level goes up.

A simple solution to eliminating this unnecessary stress is to plan on getting to all your appointments and commitments early. If you get caught in traffic or held up, you'll still be on time. And if you do actually manage to get there early, fantastic! Now you get some real YOU-time. Read a novel, meditate, review your to-do list, make those phone calls, reply to emails, or simply relax for a moment and enjoy the view.

As an added bonus, those that you are meeting with will appreciate that you value their time just as much as your time. When you are constantly tardy, it sends the wrong message to your coworkers that you don't have time management skills and/or are inconsiderate of their time.

Lighten your day (10 minutes):

Set alarms for your meetings and commitments 10 minutes earlier than you normally would. When that alarm goes off, ask yourself, "do I respect my coworkers' time?" and then make a conscious effort to get to your next meeting early.

Schedule Worry Time

(LIGHTEN™: **I**magination and **T**ime)

Do you find yourself worrying as you go to bed and then have trouble falling asleep? If so, scheduling worry time in your schedule earlier in the day or evening might be a solution.

Carve out a small chunk of time each day—ideally always at the same time and place—to focus on your worries. This way, by the time bedtime rolls around, you've already addressed everything that's making you anxious.

The key is to be productive while worrying, whether that means writing down any thoughts or concerns, creating a to-do list, or actively trying to solve the problems that the worries present. This process gives you the space to entertain your worries and then either (a) shift your focus, or (b) come up with a solution that allows you to move on.[129]

Lighten your day (15-30 minutes):

When you find yourself frequently lying awake at night worrying, consider scheduling "worry time" in your calendar for your active mind.

1. *Make sure it is scheduled at the same time and place each day.*

2. *Write down your concerns along with a to-do list that can help you solve your problems.*

3. *Once your time is up, review your notes, take a deep breath, and focus on something else.*

4. *Enjoy a more restful night's sleep.*

Enjoy Your Lunch

(LIGHTEN™: Livelihood, Health, and Time)

I know, another one of those "are you kidding me?" suggestions. What I mean by "enjoy your lunch" is do not skimp on the time you give yourself to eat properly. Wolfing down your lunch in seven minutes flat will only ramp up the stress that you bring with you from the first few hours of work. Instead, let your lunch be a time of relaxation. Eat slowly and focus on the smell, texture, and taste of the food. Put down the fork and knife down between bites to make that easier.[130]

As a bonus, you may find yourself eating fewer calories because you will give your stomach a chance to let your brain know you are full. And when you eat less, you may lose a few unwanted pounds.

> *Lighten your day (30-45 minutes):*
>
> *No matter how much work you have to do, resist the temptation to eat quickly because it just tells your body that you must be stressed. Take the time to appreciate your food. Put your utensils down between bites. Not only will you be more relaxed, you will likely consume less and potentially lose weight in the process.*

Minimize Chores
(LIGH**TE**N™: **T**ime and **E**nvironment)

Dirty dishes. Dirty laundry. Carpet needs to be vacuumed. Household chores is a part of our life, but if they are not dealt with correctly, they can become a distraction. Each time you walk into your home and see something undone, it can negatively affect your energy and cause you unnecessary stress.

Chores also have the tendency to monopolize your free time. When this happens, you lose the opportunity to relax and reflect. What's worse is that a lot of chores feel like work, and if you spend all weekend doing them, you just put in a seven-day workweek. If you cannot make the chores fun (as previously suggested), you need to schedule your chores like you would anything else during the week, and if you don't complete them during the allotted time, you move on and finish them another time.[131]

By scheduling chores in your calendar like other responsibilities, you honor that time you have allotted.

> **Lighten your day (1 hour):**
>
> *Instead of letting your household chores pile up for the weekend, schedule an hour in the evening each workday to tackle one or two. You will then find your weekends freer for fun activities that provide you with stress relief.*

Track Your Time for a Week
(LIGHTEN™: **T**ime, **E**nvironment, and **N**etwork)

A common habit many people have is thinking they have less time during the week than they actually have. This leads to unnecessary stress because we feel we have to hurry, which makes us more likely to make mistakes, further compounding our anxiety.

A good way to get a handle on the actual time you have is to objectively track it for a week and keep a notebook or spreadsheet of where you are spending your time. Track your time without actively attempting to change your behavior. Your behavior will naturally shift in positive directions due to monitoring, so there's no need to force it, at least initially.

Limit brief work-related activities during non-work time, like checking your phone or firing off a quick email. These activities may only take a few minutes, but this pattern can feel like it consumes more time than it actually does, so try to curb these behaviors. Ultimately, you want to see how much time you really are spending, not what your mind thinks you are spending when you are stressed about time.[132]

The insight that you gain from this activity will help you objectively see whether your brain jumped to conclusions based on your emotions about feeling overworked versus what actually might be true. And with this clarity about your time you can help yourself fend off unnecessary stress in the future.

Lighten your day (7 days):

When you are feeling overwhelmed at work and strapped for time, your brain can jump to conclusions based on your emotions and cause unnecessary stress. Consider tracking your activities for a week to see how much time you really are spending on work versus what your mind thinks you are spending. The week you spend tracking your time will provide you clarity and factual evidence to help you take positive action to reduce future stress.

Reflection Point

Now that we are at the end of this chapter, which stress-relief tool did you like best? What was it about the tool you liked? Making notes to yourself below will help commit what you've learned to memory:

The stress-relief tool I like best:

I will use this tool specifically for:

The one that worked best for you should be bookmarked so you can easily refer to it in the future. You can also share it with your friends and family as a way of giving back to your community. There are also video-instruction stress-relief tools available for you to review and share by visiting my blog at **PeteAlexander.com.**

What do you think happened to me that morning where I left my day planner on the roof of my car and drove off to my first appointment? Well, I jumped into my car and raced back to my apartment. One block from my house, where I made my first left, lay my day planner spread out all over the road. I pulled over and started picking up each page that I could find. I also had to catch a boy who had picked up my credit-card-size calculator. I went back to my apartment, called the customers (using 411, as my contact list was somewhere in the messed up pile of paper) letting them know I needed to reschedule, and I spent the remainder of my day trying to reconstruct my day planner.

Even though I arrived early for the meeting, as one of the time tools suggested, I should have packed my bag the night before. In this case, putting the address of the customer front and center rather than looking for it last minute, would have saved all that anxiety and the time I spent rebuilding my planner. Of course, I could have also set a boundary that I don't make sales calls earlier than 8:00 a.m. As you can see, I could have utilized three or four time-related tips for a better outcome. Lesson learned.

Interestingly, as an outside salesperson, my car was my daily office environment, and looking back, there were several things I could have done to further reduce my anxiety. If your work or home environment is causing you stress, the next chapter has some tools that can help.

You will never find time for anything. If you want time, you must make it.

—CHARLES BUXTON, ENGLISH BREWER AND PHILANTHROPIST

CHAPTER 8

ENVIRONMENT—
Tips, Tools, and Techniques for Building Yourself a Less Stressful World

You can't always control what goes on outside,
but you can always control what goes on inside.

—WAYNE DYER, AMERICAN PHILOSOPHER AND AUTHOR

I'm not a big fan of the open office plan, but not because research shows it doesn't work as intended.[133] The kind of work I do requires as much thinking time as collaborating with my coworkers. When I need time to think, even for a minute or two, I don't want to get distracted or interrupted. Unfortunately, even when I went into an empty conference room, somebody would inevitably knock on the door and say hi, or say they have the room booked. Same goes for the refuge of my car: people saw me sitting there and wondered what I was doing.

When it comes to an environment that is unsupportive, nothing tops what I saw with one of my first stress-relief clients. She was a veteran flight attendant with a major airline who, from the outside, looked like she had everything together. She dressed beautifully, she kept herself healthy and fit, and she had an exciting life traveling all over the world. Her apartment, however, was a different story.

Around the perimeter of her entire apartment were three-foot-high stacks of junk mail. Not newspapers or magazines, just good old-fashioned junk mail. Each time she went to her mailbox, she would put the junk mail on one of these stacks with the intention of reading it at some point. She would stress about throwing it out or recycling it because she believed that if the company took the time and money to send it to her, she was obligated to read it. This mail dated back several years. As the junk mail piled up, so did her anxiety to the point she didn't want to go home after a long trip.

I'll detail what we worked on to address her issue at the end of this chapter, but for now realize your environment must be supportive of your stress-relief efforts. The tips, tools, and techniques listed in this chapter are intended to help you do just that.

Remember: Each suggestion will have a key with the letter(s) highlighted in the word LIGHTEN™ to let you know that this tip, tool, or technique applies to that particular topic or topics of the model.

 = Author Uses Personally

 = Shortcut to Implementation

Appreciate the World Around You
(LIGH**TE**N™: **T**ime and **E**nvironment)

My wife Olga is a master of appreciation, and I am her avid student. Whether it is a sunset, a small chalk-written word on the ground, a heart-shaped rock, or any number of other things, she sees beauty all around us. She has taught me to be more aware of my surroundings, because that enhances my senses, and I am more likely to take notice of something amazing that life has to offer, even if it's commonplace.

Remember that old saying "stop and smell the roses?" That's what I'm suggesting here, even if it's just for a minute or less. Don't take for granted the view from your house/office, the sunshine on your face, or the flowers and trees blooming around you. You'll notice that slowing down for this short activity will have a positive effect on your stress level.

We're so busy watching out for what's just ahead of us that we don't take time to enjoy where we are.

—CALVIN & HOBBES
(AUTHOR'S ALL-TIME FAVORITE COMIC STRIP)

Lighten your day (1 minute):

On your commute to work, take one minute to notice the details of a tree, plant, the sky, or anything else that catches your attention. See if you can mentally note three details you like about that subject. That one-minute diversion will help your mind de-stress about your workday ahead.

Stress Toys
(LIGHTEN™: Livelihood, Health and Environment)

Giving your hands something to do during an anxious situation can help alleviate some of the tension. On my desk I have three toys: A mini Slinky (a metal one as the plastic ones don't work as well), a wind-up doll that looks like he is dancing to Chubby Checkers' "The Twist," and dice that humorously help me decide my next course of action.

If you attend trade shows and conferences, there is usually a vendor giving away stress balls made out of foam. Those work great to squeeze in your hand. If you do a search on **amazon.com**, there will be over 20,000 items that match the search term "stress toy."

The bottom line is that you have a large assortment to choose from. Pick something you like that puts a smile on your face and/or helps you relax.

Lighten your day (1 minute):

Google "stress toys" and pick something that appeals to you and order it. Once received, place it on your desk and pick it up any time you feel anxious or need to ponder your thoughts. You will find that giving your hands something to do while you think can help mediate a rise in your stress level.

Dammit Doll

(**LIGHTEN**™: **L**ivelihood, **I**magination, **G**enius, **H**ealth, **T**ime, **E**nvironment, and **N**etwork)

Technically, a Dammit Doll could be considered another stress toy, but the usage makes it quite different. Whereas the stress toys I mentioned above are more benign, a Dammit Doll is designed to let you release excessive negative energy. As the manufacturer describes on **amazon.com**:

> *"When life gives you that crazy urge to scream and destroy, Dammit Doll is here to support you. Go ahead – THROW, SLAM, and WHACK the ultimate stress-relief tool. The Classic Dammit Doll is engineered to absorb all that negative energy so you can let go and get your happy back on."*[134]

I actually gave one of these to my elderly mom for Christmas one year, and she whacks it against her furniture and walls every time she hears something on the news she doesn't like. It's pretty funny to watch.

Lighten your day (1 minute):

Google "Dammit Doll" and search for one that reminds you of a person or topic that agitates you and order it. Once received, slam your Dammit Doll against your desk, chair, wall, or wherever you feel the stress coming on. Of course, you will need to be discreet as to not offend your coworkers or knock anything over. Place your Dammit Doll in your bag to keep it handy any time the moment feels right to let off a little steam.

Lean Back Instead of Forward

(**LI**GHT**E**N™: **L**ivelihood, **H**ealth and **E**nvironment)

Have you noticed that when you are sitting at your desk for a long period of time your body starts to get stiff? This is especially true if you are leaning forward. When you lean back in your chair you are increasing the physical distance from a complex task and also increasing the psychological distance, which mitigates the sense of the task's difficulty. Unconsciously your mind infers that a task seen from a greater distance is easier to tackle.

It might also help to stand up and move around every 30 minutes or so to minimize the negative effects of prolonged immobility.

Give a more relaxed posture a try when working on a computer. You may even want to invest in a recliner for your office as part of your stress-relief plan.

Lighten your day (1 minute):

Set a reminder every 15-30 minutes for you to lean back and catch your breath for 30 seconds, then stand up and move around for another 30 seconds. This will help mitigate how the stress is manifesting in your body.

Aromatherapy

(**LI**GHT**E**N™: **G**enius, **H**ealth, and **E**nvironment)

Do you like the smell of vanilla? Me too. I always thought it was because I love vanilla ice cream, but clinical studies have confirmed that the smell of vanilla reduces human anxiety. In a medical study of patients undergoing a tense procedure for cancer diagnosis, a vanilla scent mixed into humidified air lessened anxiety up to 63 percent compared to patients who were administered humidified air alone.[135]

If vanilla isn't your preference, you can use essential oils to get the benefits of aromatherapy in your office. You can use an essential oil diffuser on your desk, keep a small bottle for your personal use whenever you need it, or spray the air around you by mixing it with water. If you are using an oil diffuser or sprayer, just be mindful of your coworkers who may not appreciate the aromas you have chosen.

👍 "I put lavender oil in my car air diffuser, and it keeps me calm, even when I'm stuck in traffic."

—MARIA A., CLIENT

Lighten your day (1 minute):

Buy some real vanilla extract from the grocery store. Put a few drops (or soak it if you love vanilla) on a facecloth and leave on the floor of your car or desk. Notice if the aroma helps calm you, especially when you are in traffic or stuck at your desk.

Desktop Zen Garden
(**LI**GHTEN™: **L**ivelihood, **I**magination, and **E**nvironment)

Desktop Zen gardens are designed to recreate the dry landscape gardens of Japanese Zen Buddhism on a small scale to be enjoyed in your home or office. They use rocks and gravel or sand to recreate the essence of various aspects of nature.

You can escape the stress of your busy everyday life, even for a minute, by methodically arranging the stones and combing the sand to give your mind and body the ability to relax. Focusing on the repetitive physical movements quiets your mind and enables you to truly experience the present moment, rather than worrying about the past or the future.[136]

Lighten your day (1 minute):

Google "desktop Zen garden" and order one that has the size and accessories most appealing to you. Place it on your desk and try raking sand the next time you have a challenging problem you are working on, or when you are on an especially intense conference call to help keep you focused. The more you rake, the less stressed you may become.

Minimize News Exposure

(**L**IGHTEN™: **I**magination, **G**enius, **H**ealth, **T**ime, and **E**nvironment)

The media is the business of selling news, and it is human nature to be drawn to its negative aspects. We want to know what is going on in the world, but it can have dire effects on our system.

Chronic exposure to troubling and negative news events can trigger an alarm that prompts our adrenal glands to flood our body with hormones such as cortisol and adrenaline. Our body is resilient enough to deal with passing stressors. But when the fight, flight, or freeze mode is continually triggered, our stress response may get stuck in the "on" position. We each need to get a sense of what we can handle without feeling overwhelmed or traumatized and weigh the risk of overexposure with the risk of remaining ignorant. One part of self-care is to know our boundaries in relation to how much we can expose our psyches to without feeling paralyzed or besieged.[137]

It's easy to put on the TV at home or the radio in the car and listen to news to have some background noise. However, if you are mindful of the effect (if any) negative news has on your stress levels, you might opt for a different TV show or listening to music or an audio book in your car instead.

Lighten your day (1 minute):

Negative news of the world is beyond your control, so focus on what you can control to relieve your stress: change the channel and/or put on a program that will help your mental state rather than distract and distress you.

Desk Decor
(**LI**GHT**EN**™: **L**ivelihood, **E**nvironment, and **N**etwork)

With our mobile phones, it's easy to take photos and never print them. And during stressful times at work we may not think to grab our phones and start flipping through the photos looking for ones that we like. If you have pictures of your loved ones, destinations you love, or anything that makes you smile placed around your workspace, you will be more grounded and give your area more of a personalized feel. It will also give you a constant reminder of what's important to you, which will help calm you in an otherwise anxious situation.

And if you hear a coworker bragging about their children, relationship, new car, or whatever, consider asking, "*Have I shown you a picture of my Pride and Joy?*" Then show them this for a great laugh; it works every time for me! (Image courtesy of MagicTricks.com).[138]

Lighten your day (1 minute):

Place a framed picture of your favorite person, pet, or place on your desk to help remind you of why you are working so hard. Also match that photo as a screen saver or wallpaper on your computer so you see it more often.

Paper Basketball

(**LI**GHTEN™: **L**ivelihood, **I**magination, and **E**nvironment)

This was one of my favorite stress relievers when I was younger. Try rolling up a piece of paper into a ball and play a game of HORSE with your waste basket. HORSE is a game where you sit or stand in different areas of your work space and take shots at your waste basket until you make the shot. Each letter is a different position from which to shoot from. Each time you make a basket, you earn a letter in the word HORSE. Give it a try and find out if you feel better once you have spelled HORSE. Your inner child will thank you.

One caveat: if you suck at shooting baskets, this activity will probably take more than one minute.

Lighten your day (1 minute):

Scrunch up a piece of paper into a ball, position your waste basket so you have a clear shot, imagine you are a famous basketball player, and then take your shot. Each time you make a basket, imagine a crowd of fans cheering you.

Spend Time in Nature

(LIGHTEN™: **H**ealth, **T**ime, **E**nvironment, and **N**etwork)

Do you like gardening? Going to the beach? Riding on a bike or a boat? When the dreaded stress bug bites, nature might be calling you. If you are motivated to get out in your yard, hop in your car and go to the beach, or pull out your bike from the garage I applaud you: you already know that nature works wonders on your body and mind to reduce anxiety. And a clinical study backs this up: respondents with a high amount of green space in a three kilometer radius were less affected by stressful life events than respondents with a low amount of green space in their radius.[139]

However, if you need more group support to get you motivated, then check out **meetup.com**. I found all my hiking groups here. Those groups helped me get through my divorce because I met people who were willing to listen and provide suggestions while at the same time getting out in nature. It was a real "win-win" for me.

There are groups for all kinds of nature experiences, and for all skill levels. It's a great place to find new friends and get some much-needed vitamin D.

Lighten your day (5 minutes):

Find a green belt near your work or home. Stand or sit in the grass for at least five minutes soaking up the fresh air. Let your mind wander with your eyes open or shut. Remember you can visit here any time you feel the need to destress.

Surround Yourself with Colors
(**LIGH**TEN™: **L**ivelihood, **I**magination, **G**enius, **H**ealth, and **E**nvironment)

Drab office environments with blank walls and fluorescent lighting bring me down, so I always enliven my workspace with sports pennants and memorabilia of my favorite teams and venues I have had the pleasure of seeing live. These vivid colors perked me up during the day and allowed me to have an identity within the typical office environment.

Research in neuroscience and psychology has shown the colors that we surround ourselves with on a daily basis can affect how we feel, so the choice of color in our workplaces is important.[140]

"Color psychology" looks at the properties of certain colors in relation to mood, and it has shown that green is a mood-enhancing, stress-busting color. Therefore, natural elements such as plants can help create buffers between anxiety triggers and employees.[141] I've seen this phenomenon work firsthand after installing hundreds of indoor plants in client workspaces with the interior landscaping business I have had the pleasure to own since 2005.

"I never thought putting plants in our workplace would make a difference, but the day those plants were delivered was the highlight of the quarter in our office. My coworkers love having fresh foliage, and several of them have named the plants. The plant technician who takes care of our plants has even become a part of our work family."

—Jana N., client

Lighten your day (1 hour):

Buy yourself a small plant and put it on your desk. Name your plant something fun for you to remember, and then care for it as per the instructions included in the soil stick. Greet your plant by its name in the morning and/or evening. Add other colorful elements to your work environment to perk you up and dissipate your stress.

Minimize Social Media Usage
(LIGH**TEN**™: **T**ime, **E**nvironment, and **N**etwork)

I get it: social media can be so much fun! Funny videos and finding out who's dating who or what a friend is up to can help you decompress and escape for a little while. The problem comes when that "short while" becomes a "long while."

Social media can run the gamut from being fabulously uplifting to being totally depressing and exhausting, and this applies to all ages. If you check social media at all hours of the day and night, chances are you'll complain about being tired. It impacts your sense of yourself and your identity and can make you anxious. Social media has created a new sense of impulsivity and urgency, and it can make you feel overwhelmed by what is happening in the world. These factors can be fatiguing and can impact how you sleep.[142]

The best way to ensure this doesn't happen is to limit your social media usage to one hour or less per day. As with several other suggestions in this book, consider blocking time in your calendar for your social media fix and stick to the time allotted so that you don't go overtime (otherwise you will set a bad precedent for your other calendar commitments).

> **Lighten your day (1 hour):**
>
> *If you love browsing on social media for hours on end, schedule time in your calendar to do so. Limit yourself to one hour in the evening, or 20-minute blocks three times per day. Don't let yourself go over your allotted time. Set a timer to remind you it is time to get back to the rest of your day.*

Wear a Costume to Work
(**LIGHTEN**™: **L**ivelihood, **E**nvironment, and **N**etwork)

The benefits of wearing something fun at work has amazing benefits. When you are in a costume, you get to be a persona that may remove your typical limitations or lack of confidence, especially if you struggle with being an introvert. You become much more approachable because people love creativity.

This technique can work for Halloween, your organization's holiday party, your birthday, or for any day where you think "this would be fun to wear." And it doesn't have to be an elaborate costume. Something as simple as a funny T-shirt or hat for casual Fridays can do the trick.

I've worked at many organizations throughout my career, and while I did incredible work and was a high performer, many of my former coworkers remember me most for my creative costumes. I've been known to come to work as Batman, a life-size whoopee cushion (with sound effects), a walking billboard of now-hiring ads (for our competitors' employees), Leisure Suit Larry (in 1970's tight clothes), an astronaut, Gumby (the 1960's claymation character), Dracula, an old man with suspenders and pants up to my breasts, and many, many more.

This worked so well that one of my former coworkers had this to say to me via LinkedIn: *"Pete, I think that you brought a lot of joy for all of us when you went all out at Halloween or any cool event the company was hosting. I wonder if there is a Ted Talk about the act of participating and dressing up that makes the environment more fun and friendlier at a company."*

I'm still contemplating that idea.

Lighten your day (1 hour):

Do you have a fun costume, shirt, or hat? If not, go online and order something that will appeal to your sense of humor. Then choose a day to wear it at work—Halloween, an office party, or no occasion at all—and enjoy the stress-relief benefits of making people smile.

Schedule Micro Adventures
(LIGHT**EN**™: **E**nvironment and **N**etwork)

Have you ever noticed how having something fun planned during the week can help improve your mood and lighten your stress? It's amazing what a little advanced planning can do to make your workweek less stressful.

Buy tickets to a concert or play or get reservations for that cool new hotel that just opened downtown. Instead of running on a treadmill, plan a hike. Try something you haven't done before or perhaps something you haven't done in a long time. Studies show that anticipating something good to come is a significant part of what makes the activity pleasurable. Knowing that you have something interesting planned for Saturday will not only be fun come Saturday, but it will significantly improve your mood throughout the week.[143]

The key is to get out and do something *different*—an environment you haven't been to before, or at least in a long time. Going to the same movie theater doesn't quite do it. Part of the anticipation you will have is knowing you will be in different surroundings than you are used to.

Lighten your day (1 day):

Treat yourself to a micro adventure, something that you normally wouldn't do.
Stay at a boutique hotel, visit a park you have never been to, or sign up for a weekend retreat. The anticipation of your upcoming adventure will give you something to look forward to and help reduce your stress.

Bedroom Makeover
(**LIGHTEN**™: **L**ivelihood, **H**ealth, and **E**nvironment)

So many things about a healthy and happy life (e.g., sleep, sex, relaxation) revolve around the bedroom, therefore it should have a high priority when you are designing your living space. Implement the following suggestions for developing your bedroom as a sanctuary:[144]

- Turn your bedroom into a luxury hotel suite. Think of the feeling you get when you escape to a nice hotel on vacation. Capture that in your home every day.

- Invest in comfort. Buy comfortable, quality sheets, pillows, bedding, and mattress.

- Don't skimp on window treatments. Blocking out light will help you sleep better.

- Remove the television. Bedrooms are havens for sleep, sex, and contemplation, not screen time. That also includes your phone or other electronics.

- Make the bed. Making the bed starts your day off with a small accomplishment, and you can end your day returning to a tidy, welcoming retreat.

Lighten your day (1 day):

Ensure that your bedroom supports your stress-relief efforts. Invest in comfortable sheets, pillows, bedding, a quality mattress and high-quality window coverings. Keep all electronics out, and don't forget to make your bed in the morning.

Reflection Point

Now that we are at the end of this chapter, which stress-relief tool did you like best? What was it about the tool you liked? Making notes to yourself below will help commit what you've learned to memory:

The stress-relief tool I like best:

I will use this tool specifically for:

The one that worked best for you should be bookmarked so you can easily refer to it in the future. You can also share it with your friends and family as a way of giving back to your community. There are also video-instruction stress-relief tools available for you to review and share by visiting my blog at **PeteAlexander.com.**

Circling back to my junk-mail client, we did a parts-integration process (see Genius chapter) because part of her wanted to get rid of the junk mail and part of her didn't. After the approximately 30-minute process, we discovered that she grew up in a messy household where her mother never threw anything out, and she felt that she should do the same. The process helped her realize that the junk mail wasn't serving her, and she didn't need to emulate her mother. As a result, she had a junk hauling company come pick up the unwanted mess. Once it was removed, she did a bedroom makeover (similar to what was suggested in this chapter), and her home became a relaxing place of refuge and a source of delight instead of dread.

Interesting that her mother's junk-mail habit could have had such a long-term impact on my client. There is no doubt that our relationships create stress in our lives from time to time—that's to be expected as part of the value we receive from others. However, there are tools we can utilize to minimize that anxiety, which is the subject of our next chapter.

Being in control of your life and having realistic expectations about your day-to-day challenges are the keys to stress management, which is perhaps the most important ingredient to living a happy, healthy, and rewarding life.

—Marilu Henner, American actress and author

CHAPTER 9

NETWORK—
Tips, Tools, and Techniques for Dealing with Stress Caused by Relationships

You only live once, but if you do it right,
once is enough.

—MAE WEST, AMERICAN ACTRESS

My perfect storm of 2008 had a lot to do with my network at the time. My father was in hospice care waiting to die; my mother was recovering from major surgery and needed support; my wife and I were heading for divorce; my two young children wanted my attention; and the people who reported to me at my small business needed direction. Because I didn't know how to handle the stresses of my relationships, I ended up with stress-induced diabetes.

Who you surround yourself with matters. Humans are social beings, and the quality of our relationships affects our mental, emotional, and physical health. Research shows that good relationships help people live longer, deal with stress better, have healthier habits, and have stronger resistance to colds.[145]

After my divorce, I did things differently to bring a partner into my life that helped reduce my stress rather than add to it. I'll discuss what I did to find and cultivate that relationship at the end of this chapter.

For now, realize that your coworkers, friends, family, pets and/or significant other will require you to have patience but will also give you resilience. Since you have learned earlier in this book that most stress is mental, how you deal intellectually and emotionally with those around you will go a long way with your stress-relief efforts. The following tips, tools, and techniques are designed to do just that.

Remember: Each suggestion will have a key with the letter(s) highlighted in the word LIGHTEN™ to let you know that this tip, tool, or technique applies to that particular topic or topics of the model.

 = Author Uses Personally

 = Shortcut to Implementation

Limit Contact with Negative and/or Toxic People
(**LIGHTEN**™: **L**ivelihood, **I**magination, **H**ealth, **T**ime, **E**nvironment, and **N**etwork)

Dealing with difficult people is frustrating, exhausting, and highly stressful for most. If you have to work with a negative person, try to limit the amount of time you spend interacting with him or her, whether in person, phone, or other communication method.

If avoidance is not possible, you can control your interactions with toxic people by keeping your feelings in check. When you need to confront a toxic person, approach the situation rationally. Identify your own emotions and don't allow anger or frustration to fuel the chaos. Also, try to consider the person's perspective so that you can find solutions and common ground. And if things completely derail, take the toxic person with a grain of salt to avoid letting him or her bring you down.[146]

On the flip side, try to surround yourself with positive, happy people to reduce your anxiety. Yale researchers have found the following:[147]

- People's happiness depends on the happiness of others with whom they are connected.

- A person's happiness extends to three degrees of separation, meaning that it can influence (and be influenced by) their friends, their friends' friends, and the friends of people who are friends of their friends.

- Each additional happy friend increases your chance of happiness by about 9 percent.

- Geography matters. Our happiness increases when we live close to happy friends and family members.

Bottom line: Make it a habit by hanging around happy people and avoiding negative or toxic people.

"I used to listen to my coworkers gossiping, and the negative energy of that always made me feel depressed. Now I just walk away, and I feel so much happier!"

—LINDA C., CLIENT

Lighten your day (1 minute):

When you need to engage with a negative/ toxic person, take a deep breath and resist the temptation to comment and/or encourage a negative conversation. By not encouraging the negative talk, that person will likely look for someone else to dump on and free your time for more positive activities. Also, make a conscious effort to surround yourself with positive people.

Touch Someone Close to You

(LI**GH**TEN™: Genius, Health, and Network)

When you are frustrated, worried, or any other form of stress is manifesting inside of you, a shoulder rub, simple touch or hug from someone important to you makes a big difference in relieving your anxiety. It's because we are humans, and one of our five primary senses is touch. Hugging has a particularly strong calming effect on us and reassures us that everything is going to be all right.

Scientific proof shows us that touching is one of the primary ways to release oxytocin, sometimes referred to as the "love hormone" because it elevates during hugging and orgasm. Touching someone you love has also been scientifically proven to reduce pain.[148] And giving is just as good as receiving: giving a hug to someone who needs it can also help reduce the stress you feel.

> **Lighten your day (1 minute):**
>
> Next time a friend is obviously stressed, put your hand on his/her shoulder and ask if you can help. Not only will your friend appreciate the gesture, you will also benefit because it takes the attention away from your own challenges.

Random Acts of Kindness
(**LI**GHTEN™: **L**ivelihood, **I**magination, and **N**etwork)

This is a simple yet very rewarding and effective form of stress relief. At the start of each day, take one minute to write an email or send a text praising or thanking someone you know for something they did.[149] What you are thanking them for doesn't have to be anything big: the fact that you noticed and thanked them for it can go a long way to making that person's day. This also works for friends and family you haven't connected with in a while. A simple message saying you were thinking of them works wonders.

If you have a little more time, master networker Adam Rifkin suggests his five-minute rule: every day we should do something selfless for someone else that takes under five minutes. The essence of whatever you do should be the difference it can make to the person receiving the gift. Usually these favors take the form of an introduction, reference, feedback, or shout-out on social media.[150] It can also be something like helping someone carry boxes or offering to pick up lunch or coffee for somebody who is stuck working at their desk.

Here's the caveat: don't expect a response. If you set expectations (see "Minimize Expectations" tip) you set yourself up for disappointment. Instead, send the thank-you note just because you want to. And if you do get a response, consider it the cherry on top of your ice cream sundae and enjoy a jolt of positive energy to soften any difficulties you might be experiencing.

 "I love giving people compliments and see how their faces light up—even the grumpy ones!"

—Dan R., CLIENT

Lighten your day (1 minute):

At the beginning of your workday, take one minute to send an email or text to someone thanking them or complimenting them on something they did. Make it short and sweet and don't mentally put the expectation to yourself that a response is needed.

Be Compassionate
(LIGHTEN™: Livelihood, Imagination, Health, and Network)

When we show compassion for others in need, we build a stronger ability to deal with stress ourselves.[151] As social creatures by nature, we are nurtured by support from others. Think about when you interviewed for your last job. Were you nervous? Probably. Did the person who was interviewing you do anything to calm you? Maybe not, but that would have been nice.

Being compassionate also extends to your personal time. For example, if the car in front of you has broken down, don't honk your horn in frustration. Think about what it would be like if that was you in the disabled car. Instead, just maneuver out of the way without frustration and, better still, offer to call a tow truck if you have time. When you are kind and compassionate to a stranger, your own anxiety will be mitigated.

Lighten your day (1 minute):

Be compassionate when you are interviewing someone for a job, and they are displaying obvious signs of nervousness. Offer them something to drink, take them for a short walk, and/or tell them a funny story about when you interviewed at your company. Your compassion will be appreciated.

Resist the Need to Be Liked
(**LIG**HTEN™: **L**ivelihood, **I**magination, **G**enius, and **N**etwork)

Nobody is universally liked, largely for reasons that have absolutely nothing to do with them. You are going to be liked by some, loved by others, criticized by a handful, and disliked by a few, whatever you do with your life. Therefore, it makes the most sense to do what you want, regardless of how other people will respond.[152]

If you're too caught up in others' perceptions of you in the workplace, over which you have limited control, you become stressed, and this will affect your work. Ironically, once you shift your focus from others' perception of your work to the work itself, you're more likely to impress them.[153]

This has always been a hard one for me. Growing up in a severely dysfunctional family, I always wanted my dad's approval. I didn't feel like I received it until later in life when I earned my college degrees and landed high-quality jobs. As an employee, I would frequently get uptight if somebody wasn't friendly to me. And as a professor, I would focus on the one negative student evaluation instead of the 40 highly positive ones I would receive at the end of the course.

Fortunately, I came to realize that you cannot please everyone. And with it, the burden and anxiety of not acting like myself went away. It was another important learning moment for me.

Lighten your day (1 minute):

If you get the sense that someone doesn't like you, think about someone else in your life (friends, family, coworkers, pets, etc.) who does like you. That simple mind-shift will minimize the stressful temptation to waste time getting that other person to like you.

Write Down Important Things
(**LIG**HTEN™: **L**ivelihood, **I**magination, **G**enius, and Network)

Have you ever had an important conversation with someone, and then later forgot an action item you needed to take care of? Chances are that forgetfulness created unnecessary stress in your day.

It's common knowledge that the simple act of writing things down helps you retain them over the long term. Maybe you'll decide to carry around a notebook or, if you're in a real pinch, use the notes app on your phone. Either way, remembering those little moments from your conversations with people will help you get to know them better and show that you care. You also won't stress about forgetting what was discussed.[154]

> **Lighten your day (1 minute):**
>
>
>
> *When you have a conversation with someone and your active mind thinks "I better remember that," write it down. Even if you don't have your notebook or laptop with you, use a calendar or notes app on your phone or even text or email yourself a reminder. Don't assume you will remember it later because you are asking for unnecessary stress if you forget.*

Clarify Expectations with Others

(**LI**GHTEN™: **L**ivelihood, **I**magination, **T**ime, and **N**etwork)

How many times have you expected one thing from your significant other, family, friends, or coworkers and the end result was something different? If you are like me, that has happened more times than you can remember. And chances are that some, if not most, of those unmet expectations lead to unnecessary stress.

The solution is to clarify expectations with others from the outset. Instead of assuming that your boss needs something done immediately, ask her when she needs it by. Also, be clear with people about when you'll get back to them about their request. If something will realistically take you two weeks to get to, just say so. If you don't have time to hang out with your friends or help somebody with an errand, just be honest and let them know.

This also goes for responding to texts and email messages. As discussed in the "Detox from Technology" suggestion, it does us no good to respond to messages immediately when we are on our personal time. Use an auto-responder to let people know when they can expect a response, and then practice not responding to messages outside of business hours.

Most people will get the message and may appreciate you helping them with their own boundaries.

When you limit your replies to business hours, you're more likely to consider where replying fits within your list of priorities than if your pattern is to jump to attention at any hour of the day upon receiving emails.

Lighten your day (1-5 minutes):

If you have any doubt about a deliverable that you are responsible for, don't assume you have it right. Clarify expectations with others to ensure you deliver as expected, avoiding unnecessary stress in the process.

"Chunking" Communication

(**LI**GHTE**N**™: **L**ivelihood, **I**magination, and **N**etwork)

Effective communication is an important skill to help us maintain a healthy stress level because it allows us to have quality conversations while also staying on schedule. However, we may need to interact with individuals who are either "stuck in the weeds" with too many details or "high flyers" who don't provide any details that allow you to support them. Both types can be a time-suck, especially if you have to pull out the necessary information you need to do your job.

This is where "chunking" can help. When someone is providing you way more detail than you need, consider asking them the question "what is this an example of?" or "for what purpose is this?" This gets the individual to break up their thinking into more manageable "chunks" and allows them to get to the important issue faster.

On the other hand, when somebody isn't providing you the details you need, consider asking "what are examples of this?" or "what specifically...?"

Again, these questions encourage the individual to "chunk" their thinking down and provide more specific details so you can take action or provide feedback as needed.

Lighten your day (5 minutes):

When you find yourself in a conversation with someone who is providing too many details, ask them "what is this an example of?" to get them to think about their issue in higher level chunks. If you are in a conversation with someone who isn't providing enough detail, ask them "what are examples of this?" to get more specific details you may need. This will allow you to effectively communicate with these individuals and minimize your stress by not wasting time trying to get to the point of the conversation.

Don't Hold Grudges
(LIGHTEN™: **I**magination, **H**ealth, and **N**etwork)

The person who bullied you in school. The lover who dumped you for somebody else. The boss who promoted your peer instead of you ... the list of people you hold grudges against could get long and ugly.

The negative emotions that come with holding onto a grudge are, in fact, a stress response. Just thinking about the event may send your body into fight-or-flight mode, a survival mechanism that forces you to stand up and fight or run for the hills when faced with a threat. When the threat is imminent, this reaction is essential to your survival, but when the threat is ancient history, holding onto that stress wreaks havoc on your body and can have devastating health consequences over time (refer to the "What's Stress Costing You?" chapter for additional information).

Holding onto a grudge means you're holding onto stress, and emotionally intelligent people know to avoid this at all costs. Letting go of a grudge not only makes you feel better now but can also improve your health.[155]

The fact is that you cannot please everyone; inevitably, you will have an encounter with one or more people who rub you the wrong way. If you have any lingering emotions from that encounter, get into the habit of keeping a list of what negative encounters you experienced during the day so you can take care of that at night.

In the evening, before you go to bed, review your list and those people who were involved. Close your eyes and imagine that person facing you. Look them in the eyes and say, "I forgive you. Please forgive me, too." This process stems from the Hawaiian practice called Ho'oponopono. There are meditations available that can guide you through the process simply by Googling Ho'oponopono, just make sure you get the spelling right! Ho'oponopono helps you imagine that you are forgiving the person you are holding a grudge against, and that person forgiving you too. This process restores harmony within yourself by eliminating the stress and resentment you have been directing at that person.[156]

"Before resigning from my job, I did Ho'oponopono meditation. Things went super easy the next day at work. My boss even gave me a hug, and she's not a touchy-feely person."

—RACHAEL R., CLIENT

Lighten your day (5-10 minutes):

If you have had a negative encounter with someone during the day, write it down and then use the following process to remove any lingering negative emotions or stress:

1. *Before you go to bed, review what you wrote down and recall those who were involved.*

2. *Close your eyes and imagine that person facing you. Look them in the eyes and say to them, "I forgive you. Please forgive me, too."*

3. *Imagine that person giving you a sign that they have forgiven you.*

4. *Repeat as necessary for any other people involved in the negative encounter.*

5. *When completed, take a deep breath and open your eyes. You should feel a sense of relief.*

Get a Venting Partner
(L**I**GHTEN™: **I**magination, **H**ealth, and **N**etwork)

Venting is a great way to manage stress, especially if it allows you to express your frustration rather than play the blame game (refer to the "Avoid the Victim Mentality" technique for a refresher on why). And as the old saying goes, "It takes two to tango."

You need to have somebody you can talk to so that you can get things off your chest and experience a cathartic release. However, you should only call someone who you know will be supportive of you, or you will end up even more irritated.[157]

A venting partner is there to listen to you without judgment, allowing you to share your problem and release steam. Your venting partner can then help you find a solution to your problem, if appropriate, once you have calmed down and released some of your anxiety. Having a go-to person who is not involved in the situation listen to your frustration allows you to get the benefits of stress relief without jeopardizing the relationship you have with the person or people who initially caused you to become agitated.

If your venting partner needs to vent themselves, offer them the opportunity to do so and give them your full attention, otherwise your relationship will be one-sided, unbalanced, and likely to falter over time.

Lighten your day (10 minutes):

Seek out a go-to person who you can talk to when you need to vent. This could be a coworker, family member, or friend. Just be sure that you use this opportunity to express your frustration rather than placing blame (refer to the "Avoid the Victim Mentality" technique), and make sure it is someone who will be supportive of you.

Healing Figure
(**LIGHTEN**™: **I**magination, **G**enius, and **N**etwork)

We all have at least one person in our lives that continuously challenges us, right? The horrible boss, family member, neighbor, coworker, or customer who causes us grief. And if your life was a movie, your main character might get a voodoo doll and stick pins in that difficult person to cause them pain.

Well, this recommendation is not voodoo, as I learned from my friend Tracy Appleton.[158] Rather, it is a healing figure that can be just about anything you want it to be—a little doll, a stuffed animal, a figurine—whatever symbolizes the person you have in your mind.

Once you have this figure, place it in a nice bag similar to one that holds jewelry or a special gift. Write down three to five positive words you would like to send that person (I suggest considering forgiveness as one of them). Each time you feel anxiety as a result of this person, review your list and hold the figure in its special container until your stressful feelings subside.

Lighten your day (10-15 minutes):

If you have someone important in your life who is causing you stress, try the following:

1. Google "small figurines" and order one that reminds you of that person. Also order a small gift bag to place it in.

2. Write down three to five positive words you would like to send this person (forgiveness might be one of them) and place your list inside the bag with the figurine.

3. Place your bagged figurine in your purse or backpack.

4. Each time you feel anxiety because of this person, pull out the bag, review your list, and hold the figurine in its bag as you repeat your words to yourself until your negative feelings subside.

Practice Active, Nonjudgmental Listening

(LIGHTEN™: **I**magination and **N**etwork)

Have you ever spoken to someone who wouldn't let you finish before they began to speak over you, arguing their point? They weren't listening at all. Whether it is your friends, family, or coworkers, people who don't listen and like to argue typically have high "self-orientations" and low "trust equations."

The trust equation says that your trustworthiness to others is based on a formula that takes your perceived credibility, reliability and intimacy with others and divides those numbers (based on a scale of 1-10) by your self-orientation score (the number others perceive as you doing things for your own personal gain). The higher the self-orientation, the lower your perceived trustworthiness.[159]

Listening builds trust. When we listen—that is, truly listen—to someone, we communicate that they are important to us and have something valuable to contribute. And it should be in a receptive, nonjudgmental manner.

When people listen without judgment to each other, they set the stage to receive feedback they can't receive in any other way. Even if you have limited time with someone, look them in the eye, be totally present with that person and listen to what they have to say.[160] Not only will you build rapport with this person, you will clearly understand their issues and minimize the chance for misinterpretations and potential additional stress.

Lighten your day (10-60) minutes:

When you have a one-on-one conversation, put down your phone and close your laptop so that you give that person your full attention. Try not to judge what the person is saying and just listen. You both will benefit from you being fully present and objective.

Delegate Important Work
(LIGHTEN™: Imagination, Time, and Network)

The higher up you are in an organization, the more responsibility you have for important work that falls squarely on your shoulders, and with it comes additional stress.

A great way to handle this is to properly delegate work to others. Effectively delegating doesn't mean dumping work on somebody else. It means selecting capable individuals and providing clear direction. Otherwise, delegating will give you more stress, not less.

The amount of authority you relinquish should match the skill and readiness of the person to whom you're delegating the task. It should begin with a clear conversation between you and the employee to clarify expectations, honestly assess what the employee is ready to take on, and explain how you will remain involved. Too often, a sense of urgency causes leaders to skip this important preparation. In fact, the more urgent a project is, the more carefully planned the delegated authority must be.[161]

If you are going to delegate, do it right.

Lighten your day (1 hour):

Delegate projects to someone who is capable of handling the extra work. Ensure success for both you and the other person by providing clear direction and expectations. Effectively delegating improves your leadership skills while also reducing your stress.

Communicating Bad News

(**LI**GHTEN™: **L**ivelihood and **N**etwork)

We've all been in the position of having to communicate bad news to others. It probably started with being a child when you broke something or did something you weren't supposed to and got caught. As an adult, the stakes are higher: you need to break up with your significant other or you need to lay off an employee. Whatever the situation might have been, it likely skyrocketed your stress prior to and during that conversation.

It doesn't have to be that way. If you spend time carefully crafting messages that blend the right degree of diplomacy and directness, tailored to those hearing it, the other person will be far better prepared to deal with what comes afterward. Identify your own discomfort with their defensiveness or anger, then write out the message in clear, nonjudgmental language in no more than two to three sentences. Then deliver the message within the first two minutes of the conversation: no long build-ups, no small talk to delay or warm up. Use the remainder of the conversation to process your message by allowing the recipient to ask questions, vent, or clarify. Make it about their needs, not yours.[162]

Lighten your day (1 hour):

When you need to have a difficult conversation, write out the message ahead of time in clear, nonjudgmental language in no more than two to three sentences. Deliver it at the beginning of the conversation and use the remainder of the conversation to allow the other person to process and respond to what they have heard. Be compassionate and make the conversation about their needs. Chances are the conversation will go better than you expect, and you will minimize your stress in the process.

Seek Advice
(**LI**GHTEN™: **L**ivelihood, **I**magination, and **N**etwork)

I know it is tempting to try and figure out everything for yourself. That can be effective if you have the available time and energy, but what if you don't? What if you have no clue how to handle a particular situation? Just thinking about that will cause you anxiety.

If you are like me, stress shuts your thinking process down. You tend to hold fixed ideas about how you think things in life should turn out, and fixed ideas about how you want them to turn out. However, these fixed ideas may be in opposition to how things are going in reality.

When you cannot get yourself out of a painful rut, it is wise to seek advice from others who are more experienced. This outside advice can do wonders when it comes to opening your mind and making you feel less alone and more supported. We all need support. People want to help other people. All you have to do is put your ego down, ask for the help you need and remain open to new ways of thinking.[163]

Lighten your day (1 hour):

When you find yourself struggling with the solution to a problem, reach out to your network of friends and/or coworkers who have experience in this area. If you don't have somebody in mind, consider asking your friends/coworkers if they have somebody they could recommend or Google a professional coach with a background similar to yours who can help you find a solution.

Spend Time in Groups
(LIGHTEN™: **H**ealth and **N**etwork)

Ever notice how we tend to isolate ourselves when we are stressed out? Belonging to groups, such as networks of friends, family, clubs, and sport teams improves mental health because they provide support, help you to feel good about yourself, and keep you active. Interestingly, people with multiple group memberships cope better when faced with stressful situations and are even more likely to stay healthy when exposed to the cold virus.[164] An unlikely cure for the common cold!

If your professional life is causing you the most stress, consider reaching out and joining a professional association related to your line of work. You can attend meetings and interact with others coping with the same workplace demands and potentially form smaller "Mastermind" groups with others looking for ongoing support and collaboration.

On a personal level, one of the best ways to find new friends and groups of like-minded individuals is **meetup.com**, as I've mentioned previously. There are groups for almost anything you can think of. A simple keyword search on this site for something that interests you will list all the relevant groups nearest to where you live. You can join multiple groups and see which ones you like best. And if you don't find a group specific to your interest, consider starting a group yourself so that you can attract other folks with similar interests to you.

👍 "I love hiking, and I love meeting new people and making friends. Joining a hiking group makes my life more fun and fulfilling. I even found my true love in one of the groups. It was like we dated 100 times on scheduled hikes before actually going out together as a couple for the first time."

—ED K., CLIENT

Lighten your day (3-4 hours):

*Set up a free account on **meetup.com**. Do a keyword search on an activity you enjoy. Join a group that matches that activity and sign up for one of their upcoming meetups. Commit to attending, even if you don't feel like going.*

Reflection Point

Now that we are at the end of this chapter, which stress-relief tool did you like best? What was it about the tool you liked? Making notes to yourself below will help commit what you've learned to memory:

The stress-relief tool I like best:

I will use this tool specifically for:

The one that worked best for you should be bookmarked so you can easily refer to it in the future. You can also share it with your friends and family as a way of giving back to your community. There are also video-instruction stress-relief tools available for you to review and share by visiting my blog at **PeteAlexander.com**.

★ ★ ★

For those of you wondering what I did to find the person of my dreams after my divorce, here's the inside scoop. I asked for advice from others, and the main suggestion I implemented was to write down my "must have" qualities in my significant other and limited that list to five. Those five were emotional intimacy, a love of nature, physically fit/attractive, a great sense of humor, and self-motivation. I figured anything more would make it difficult to find the right person. Everything that was not on that list I considered unimportant.

I then started participating in meetup groups, and sure enough I met my significant other at one in Washington State and we exchanged phone numbers. Each time we spoke, I practiced active, non-judgmental listening because I wanted to get to know her and make sure she had all of my "must haves." In addition, we were creative about maintaining our long-distance relationship, utilizing technology to help us stay connected on date nights when we were physically 800 miles apart.

As our relationship blossomed, I still had one big stressor I needed to deal with: my ex-wife. I was holding a grudge against her for mentally abandoning our 20-year marriage. Through a lot of personal work, I realized that we were both happier apart then we were together, and I was able to release that grudge and negative emotion tied to it. Once I was over that hurdle, it was just a matter of time before I proposed to my girlfriend, and we married in 2018.

I am a very rich person indeed—not because of money, but because I have a wealth of friends and family that love me. Challenges will frequently come with my network, yet how I handle that anxiety makes all the difference in the quality of those relationships. Don't take your network for granted. Manage your stress effectively, and your network will appreciate you even more.

Now that we have come to the end of the LIGHTEN™ Model components, the next chapter provides a quick reference table you can refer to any time you need a fast and easy stress-relief tool for when shit happens.

There's going to be stress in life, but it's your choice whether to let it affect you or not.

—VALERIE BERTINELLI, AMERICAN ACTRESS

CHAPTER 10

Tips, Tools, and Techniques Quick Reference Guide

Life is really simple, but we insist on making it complicated.

—CONFUCIUS, CHINESE TEACHER AND PHILOSOPHER

There are a lot of tips, tools, and techniques included in this book, so the following table lists each one for your convenience. In addition to categorizing them by their most applicable category of the LIGHTEN™ Model, they are sorted by the approximate amount of time (clock) you will need to conduct the activity. The table also marks whether it should be an ongoing activity for you and includes the book page number where you can find the instructions on how to use the tool.

If you have an idea for how to further categorize these tips in a way that would be helpful to you, please let me know by contacting me at **PeteAlexander.com**. I'll be sure to credit you just like I have all the other sources included in this book.

Title	L	I	G	H	T	E	N	Clock	Ongoing?	Page Number
Gratitude	X			X		X	X	1 minute	X	27
Smiling & Sunglasses			X	X		X	X	1 minute		114
Visualization	X	X		X	X	X	X	1 minute		55
Deep Breathing	X			X	X	X	X	1 minute		111
Laughter		X		X			X	1 minute		112
Proper Nutrition				X				1 minute	X	113
Limit Contact with Negative and/or Toxic People	X	X		X	X	X	X	1 minute		175
Set Boundaries	X				X		X	1 minute		139
Touch Someone Close to You			X	X			N	1 minute		176
Understand Busy Does Not Equal Success	X	X			X			1 minute		141
Don't Multitask	X	X	X		X			1 minute	X	28
Ask the Pendulum		X	X					1 minute		84
Avoid the Victim Mentality		X	X					1 minute		90
Appreciate the World Around You					X	X		1 minute		157
Your Perception Is Your Reality	X	X	X	X	X	X	X	1 minute	X	86
Avoid Ruminating		X	X	X				1 minute		83
Keep Your Head Up		X	X	X				1 minute	X	115
Be Compassionate	X	X		X			X	1 minute	X	178
It's Either Hell Yes! or No		X	X					1 minute		91

Title	L	I	G	H	T	E	N	Clock	Ongoing?	Page Number
Understand That Money Equals Life Energy	X	X		X	X	X		1 month		49
Remember the Lottery		X			X			1 minute	X	56
Traction				X				1 minute	X	116
Temple Touch				X				1 minute		117
Paper Basketball	X	X				X		1 minute		164
Expect a Magnificent Outcome	X	X		X	X	X	X	1 minute	X	57
Repeating Mantras		X				X		1 minute		57
Stress Toys	X			X		X		1 minute		158
Dammit Doll	X			X		X	X	1 minute		159
Talk to Yourself		X	X					1 minute		87
Lean Back Instead of Forward	X			X		X		1 minute		160
Aromatherapy		X	X			X		1 minute		160
Don't Try to Control the Uncontrollable	X	X				X	X	1 minute		58
Avoid Intoxication		X	X	X				1 minute	X	118
Reframe Failing	X	X						1 minute		60
Shake It Off	X	X		X		X		1 minute		119
End-of-Day Anchor	X	X			X	X		1 minute	X	30
Affirmations		X	X	X				1 minute		88
Slow Down	X				X	X	X	1 minute	X	142

Title	L	I	G	H	T	E	N	Clock	Ongoing?	Page Number
Resist the Need to Be Liked	X	X	X				X	1 minute		179
One-Minute Rule	X				X	X		1 minute	X	143
Reframe Your Fear		X	X					1 minute		89
Scream into a Pillow				X		X		1 minute		119
Dark Chocolate				X				1 minute		120
Desktop Zen Garden	X	X				X		1 minute		161
Email Purge	X						X	1 minute		31
Watch an Animal Video!		X						1 minute		61
Label Your Stress		X	X					1 minute		92
Minimize News Exposure		X	X	X	X	X		1 minute		162
Minimize Unproductive Meetings	X				X		X	1 minute		144
Unsubscribe from Mailing Lists	X	X			X			1 minute	X	62
Write Down Important Things	X	X					X	1 minute		180
Unconsciously Ponder a Problem	X	X	X		X			1 minute		103
Realize Work Expands	X				X			1 minute		140
Desk Decor	X					X	X	1 Minute		163
Clench Your Bottom	X			X				1-2 minutes		121
Be Mindful of Food on Business Trips	X			X			X	1-5 minutes		124
Have More Sex				X			X	At least 3 minutes :)	X	125

Title	L	I	G	H	T	E	N	Clock	Ongoing?	Page Number
Random Acts of Kindness	X	X					X	1-5 Minutes	X	177
Clarify Expectations with Others	X	X			X		X	1-5 Minutes		181
Take Care of Your Skin			X	X	X			1-5 Minutes	X	122
Singing		X		X	X	X		1-5 Minutes		123
Spend Time in Nature				X	X	X	X	5 minutes		165
Hakalau	X	X	X				X	5 minutes		92
Find Something Nostalgic			X					5 minutes		94
The Declipse Habit		X				X	X	5 minutes		63
Meditation		X	X	X		X		5 minutes		64
Listen to Music		X	X		X	X		5 minutes		94
Plan Your Day	X	X			X		X	5 minutes	X	145
Chew Gum	X			X			X	5 minutes		121
Prioritize Tasks	X	X		X	X		X	5 minutes	X	33
Pack Your Bag the Night Before	X				X			5 minutes	X	146
"Chunking" Communication	X	X					X	5 minutes		182
Emotional Freedom Technique		X	X	X				5 minutes		95
Roll Out Your Stress				X		X		5-10 minutes		125
Turn Your Dream into a Goal		X	X		X			5-10 minutes		97
Don't Hold Grudges		X		X			X	5-10 Minutes	X	183
Arrive Early to Meetings	X				X		X	10 minutes	X	147

Title	L	I	G	H	T	E	N	Clock	Ongoing?	Page Number
Exercise			X					10 Minutes	X	126
Minimize Expectations	X	X					X	10 Minutes		65
S.T.O.P. Method	X	X		X			X	10 Minutes		66
Shower for Body and Mind		X		X				10 Minutes		127
Drink More Water			X					10 Minutes	X	127
Take Microbreaks	X	X					X	10 Minutes		34
Get a Venting Partner		X		X			X	10 Minutes		185
Create Your Ideal Day	X	X			X	X		10-15 Minutes		70
Play Fact or Fiction		X	X					10-15 Minutes		67
Healing Figure		X	X				X	10-15 minutes		186
Forgive Your Past		X	X	X			X	10-30 minutes		98
Journaling	X	X	X				X	15-30 minutes		69
Weekly Reflection	X	X						15-30 minutes	X	36
Schedule Worry Time		X		X				15-30 minutes		148
Coloring or Doodling		X	X					15-30 minutes		71
Take a Power Nap	X	X	X	X	X	X	X	20-30 minutes		128
Play Relaxing Sounds		X	X		X	X		30 minutes		99
Trauma Release Exercises		X	X	X				30 minutes		131
Grounding Through Earthing		X	X	X		X		30 minutes		129
Practice Active, Nonjudgmental Listening		X					X	10-60 Minutes	X	188

Title	L	I	G	H	T	E	N	Clock	Ongoing?	Page Number
Enjoy Your Lunch	X			X	X			30-60 Minutes	X	149
Parts Integration	X	X	X	X	X	X	X	30-60 Minutes		100
Allow Yourself to Be Bored	X	X		X	X	X		30-60 Minutes		72
Read a Good Book		X			X	X		30-60 Minutes		73
Hobbies		X					X	1 hour	X	74
Detox from Technology	X	X		X	X	X	X	1 hour	X	36
Realize You Can't Do It All	X			X		X		1 hour		38
Surround Yourself with Colors	X	X	X	X		X		1 hour		166
Minimize Chores				X	X			1 hour	X	150
Delegate Important Work	X			X		X		1 hour		189
Communicating Bad News	X					X		1 hour		190
Communicate Workplace Stresses to Your Employer	X					X	X	1 hour		38
Minimize Social Media Usage				X	X	X		1 hour	X	167
Overcome Imposter Syndrome	X					X		1 hour		39
Get a Massage			X		X			1 hour	X	132
Discover Your Personality		X				X		1 hour		75
Determine Your Personal Values	X	X	X	X	X	X	X	1 hour	X	101
Decide to Stay or Quit Your Job	X	X	X	X		X	X	1 hour		41
Map Your "Ikigai"	X	X		X	X			1 hour		43

Title	L	I	G	H	T	E	N	Clock	Ongoing?	Page Number
Create Your Joy List	X	X	X	X	X	X	X	1 hour		76
Wear a Costume to Work	X					X	X	1 hour		168
Seek Advice	X	X					N	1 hour		191
Write a Personal Mission Statement	X	X		X		X	X	1 hour		45
Develop Your Passion	X	X	X	X	X	X	X	1 hour		47
Spend Time in Groups				X			X	A few hours		192
Vision Board or Binder	X	X	X	X		X	X	A few hours		77
Write Your Own Eulogy	X	X		X	X		N	4 hours		79
Get Good Quality Sleep	X	X	X	X	X	X	X	6-8 hours	X	132
Schedule Micro Adventures		X				X	X	1 day	X	169
Mental and Emotional Release (MER)	X	X	X	X	X	X	X	1 day		104
Bedroom Makeover		X		X		X		1 day		170
Track Your Time for a Week	X	X			X	X	X	1 week		151
Understand That Money Equals Life Energy	X	X		X	X	X		1 month		50

If I make a wrong decision, I worry what might have been. I stress out over very insignificant things.

—COURTNEY BARNETT, AUSTRALIAN SINGER AND SONGWRITER

CONCLUSION

Who's Going to Win ...
You or Your Stress?

When we commit to action, to actually doing
something rather than feeling trapped by events,
the stress in our life becomes manageable.

—GREG ANDERSON, AMERICAN AUTHOR

When I am working with a client or presenting on the subject of stress relief, I often get asked which tools have worked best for me. I have tried each of the tools discussed in this book at least once, and of the 100-plus I have experimented with and written about, more than 40 have had a significant effect on helping me reduce my stress.

Stress Relief Tools I Use Regularly

LIVELIHOOD. I list what I am grateful for every night with my partner. It is a great way to recap what went right about our day. I prioritize my tasks at the beginning of my workday, and I have an end-of-day anchor (my wife returning from work) that signals that I must now wrap up for the day. I also take microbreaks every 60 to 90 minutes when I refill my water, go to the restroom, and/or stretch. Finally, I continue developing my passion for stress relief, figuring out ways to help spread the word so that others can benefit from these amazing tools.

IMAGINATION. I often visualize what a magnificent outcome would be for whatever is planned for the day, and my vision binder is a great reminder of what I am working towards as I pursue my utopia. I often remind myself that I have won the lottery (figuratively) and that failure is just feedback on the way to success. I unsubscribe to legitimate email lists when I determine they are no longer relevant to me, and I frequently play fact or fiction whenever an assumption is bothering me. And of course, I love concentrating on my hobbies, as it is a way to find "me" time.

GENIUS. My unconscious genius helps me make decisions, whether they be short-term by asking the pendulum or long-term by comparing the decision to my top personal values. I use Hakalau to calm me before an important presentation; I listen to music when I am in traffic to distract me from thinking how much time I'm wasting; and I have used the power of the written letter to let go of negative emotions I have been carrying towards a particular individual. Understanding that my perception is my reality has been enlightening for me, and my experience with mental and emotional release (MER) has been nothing short of life-changing.

HEALTH. I continue to make health my priority, starting my day with a combined deep breathing/meditation exercise, and I then check my newsfeed for humorous items to encourage me and my network to laugh. I remind myself to keep my head up when I walk, and I smile at strangers I make eye contact with (I get a smile back around 50 percent of the time). I use my pull-up bar every day to stretch my back, I exercise every other day at the gym, and yes, I constrict my anus 100 times as part of my stretching regime (ha ha!). My wife and I enjoy regular sex together, and I practice trauma release exercises 1 or 2 times per week. I try to drink 100 ounces of water each day, and I do my best to get 8 hours of quality sleep each night.

TIME. To help me gain back some time, I set proper boundaries because I understand that my work will expand to the time I give it. Therefore, as I plan my day, I block out hours in my calendar for important things unrelated to my profession to ensure work doesn't take over. I also continue to arrive early for meetings, keeping my reputation as a punctual person intact.

ENVIRONMENT. In my work area, I often play with my stress toys during conference calls and look at my pictures and motivational signs to keep things in perspective. I love dressing up in either costumes or ridiculous clothing to make people laugh. I love to schedule micro-adventures with my friends and family, and I take every opportunity I can to be out in nature and breathe the fresh air.

NETWORK. I have continued to cultivate my network by limiting my contact with negative and toxic people and focusing on a community of friends, family, peers, and coworkers who positively support each other. If I do have a negative encounter, I use Ho'oponopono at the end of my day to clear my mind. I hug my friends and family when I see them, and I like to conduct random acts of kindness whenever the inspiration hits me. I make sure to put important notes, tasks, and appointments into my phone so I don't forget them. I serve as a venting partner with my close friends and family, and I'm not afraid to seek advice from those more knowledgeable than me when the need arises. I also love spending time with my hiking groups.

Yes, those are a lot of tools I use regularly, and I continue to be an eager student to try new approaches as I find out about them. That's part of being a life-long learner and the main reason I included a recommended reading list in the next chapter so you can do the same.

As you think back about the tips in each chapter, which one did you choose as your favorite to write down at the end of the chapter? Will you commit it to habit and use it as often as you need? Will you share it with your friends and family who could also benefit from a little less stress? Please share the wealth you have learned with your network.

Difficulty Getting Started?

If you haven't tried any of the tools yet, what's holding you back?

We are all busy with our careers, our personal lives, you name it. Time is a valuable resource and why one of the chapters of this book (and a core element of the LIGHTEN™ Model) is dedicated to helping you manage your stress as it relates to time. Remember that the primary purpose of this book is to provide a resource for getting easy and effective stress relief in just a few minutes per day.

The majority of the stress relief tips, tools, and techniques included within these pages will take you five minutes or less to complete. Even better, a large percentage of the tools discussed only require one minute of your time. By focusing even just one minute a day on stress relief, you can expect one or more of the following results:[165]

- You will find energy you didn't know you had, because it's a chance for your body to reset and recharge.

- You will find time you didn't know you had. Stress causes you to focus on things you can't control or can't change. Living without this anxiety will allow you to focus on the things you really care about.

- Your creativity will blossom. As mentioned previously, reducing stress increases energy and helps people manage their time more effectively. Creative people have been known to focus their anxiety into their art.

- Your self-care will increase. Just like stress causes you to focus on things you can't change, it zaps your energy and steals your desire to take care of yourself. Your health is paramount. Remember: without your health, it is hard to do anything else. Stress relief helps you align your most important priorities.

Don't make the mistake I made and let stress lower the quality of your life to the point that you end up in the hospital. Be proactive and pick a tool that you think would be interesting to try, and then do it! If that first tool doesn't work, try another one that sounds good. Keep trying different techniques until you find a tool or two that works for you and stick with those.

And don't procrastinate. Convince yourself that a couple minutes a day is a fair trade for the mental and physical health that will come from winning the battle against negative stress.

Next Steps

If the above benefits listed don't convince you to try even a single one-minute technique, work with a coach who can help motivate you and keep you accountable. Coaches can work with you for one or weekly sessions depending on what works best for you needs and schedule. Working with a coach helps in the following ways:

- Understanding what your stress response is physically, mentally and emotionally;

- Identifying your stress "triggers" that consistently put you in that fight-or-flight response and how this relates to your thoughts, moods, and energy;

- Learning and practicing techniques that work to create long-term, systemic change in your stress levels, and

- Holding you accountable for keeping your commitment to making positive changes in how you deal with whatever is thrown at you as shit happens.

You can learn more about stress-relief coaching at **PeteAlexander.com**. There are also video-instruction stress relief tools available for you to review and share by visiting my blog at **PeteAlexander.com**.

Whatever you choose to do, the important thing is to take action against your stress. Your mind and body will thank you for it.

Whether you think you can, or you think you can't—you're right.

—Henry Ford, founder of the Ford Motor Company

Recommended Reading

The secret of change is to focus all of your energy
not on fighting the old, but on building the new.

—Socrates, Greek philosopher

You've probably noticed that I have cited a lot of sources in this book, which you can find in the Endnotes section. All of those cited resources would be recommended reading if you have the time. However, if you want to read some books that truly influenced my attitude about stress and how to deal with it constructively, then check out one or more of the following books.

Rhonda Byrne. *The Magic.* The book that taught me the true power of gratitude. The author takes you through daily exercises in all aspects of your life to change your perspective and help you create a mindset of gratefulness so that the universe can help you achieve whatever it is you want in life.

John M. Gottman and Nan Silver. *The Seven Principles for Making Marriage Work.* This book has a bunch of activities to keep your relationship healthy. It helped me determine that my first marriage was irreparable, and it also reinforced that my second marriage was right for me.

Mark Manson. *The Subtle Art of Not Giving A F★CK.* I like the author's humor as he makes his primary point: that improving our lives hinges not on our ability to turn lemons into lemonade, but on learning to better stomach lemons, just like stress-relief tips and tools are intended to teach you how to better manage your anxiety.

Greg McKeown. *Essentialism - The Disciplined Pursuit of Less.* The author suggests using a more selective criteria for determining what is essential for you to get done. This process allows you to make the highest possible contribution towards the things that really matter. This is a must-read if you feel stretched too thin and/or busy but not productive.

Jeff Olson. *The Slight Edge.* The author teaches you a simple way of processing information that enables you to make the daily choices that will lead you to the success and happiness you desire. Amazingly, most people choose not to think this way, which gives those who do the slight edge.

Neil Pasricha. *The Happiness Equation.* The author describes his nine secrets to happiness that are based on a common ideal, flips it on its head, and then casts it in a completely new light along with step-by-step instructions on how to apply each secret to your life.

Vicki Robin, Joe Dominguez. *Your Money or Your Life: 9 Steps to Transforming Your Relationship with Money and Achieving Financial Independence.* As we know, money has a way of affecting all aspects of our life. If you are struggling financially and money is as the root of a lot of your stress, get this book and learn how to gain control of your finances and the freedom that comes with it.

Hal Urban. *Life's Greatest Lessons - 20 Things That Matter.* If you have young adults at home, this book is a must. If you don't, it's still a great refresher. Some of the topics the author covers include the importance of attitude, hard work, honesty, the choices we make, and what success really looks like.

Twenty years from now you will be more disappointed by the things you didn't do than by the ones you did do. So, throw off the bowlines. Sail away from the safe harbor. Catch the trade winds in your sails. Explore. Dream. Discover.

—MARK TWAIN, AMERICAN WRITER AND HUMORIST

Endnotes

1   https://www.linkedin.com/in/petealexander/

2   Alexander, P. - "Break the Cycle of Family Dysfunction": https://www.youtube.com/watch?v=d7HGzLMddHM

3   Bradberry, T. – "Stress Literally Shrinks Your Brain (How to Reverse the Damage)" - https://www.govexec.com/excellence/promising-practices/2015/12/stress-literally-shrinks-your-brain-how-reverse-damage/124626/

4   Carucci, R. – "Stress Leads to Bad Decisions. Here's How to Avoid Them" - https://hbr.org/2017/08/stress-leads-to-bad-decisions-heres-how-to-avoid-them

5   The American Institute of Stress – "Workplace Stress" - https://www.stress.org/workplace-stress

6   Cook, D. – "Workplace Stress Costing Employers $500 Billion Annually" - https://www.benefitspro.com/2017/10/20/workplace-stress-costing-employers-500-billion-ann/

7   White, G. – "The Alarming, Long-Term Consequences of Workplace Stress" - https://www.theatlantic.com/business/archive/2015/02/the-alarming-long-term-consequences-of-workplace-stress/385397/

8   Hanks, H. – "Stress and the 10 Truths Behind the Damage It Causes" - https://healthprep.com/living-healthy/stress-and-the-10-truths-behind-the-damage-it-causes/

9   Matthews, M. - "8 Ways That Stress Shows on Your Face: The Aging Effects of Anxiety" - https://www.medicaldaily.com/8-ways-stress-shows-your-face-aging-effects-anxiety-411889

10 Cleveland Clinic - "What Happens When Your Immune System Gets Stressed Out?" - https://health.clevelandclinic.org/what-happens-when-your-immune-system-gets-stressed-out/

11 Iliades, C. - "How Stress Affects Digestion" - https://www.everydayhealth.com/wellness/united-states-of-stress/how-stress-affects-digestion/

12 Breeze, J. - "Can Stress Cause Weight Gain?" - https://www.webmd.com/diet/features/stress-weight-gain

13 https://www.vox.com/2016/8/31/12368246/obesity-america-2018-charts

14   Rock, D. (2008). SCARF: A Brain-Based Model for Collaborating With and Influencing Others. NeuroLeadership Journal, (1) 1, pgs. 296-320.

15   White, R.C. (2018). The Stress Management Workbook. Althea Press, pgs. 18-22.

16   Pryce-Jones, J. "Happiness at Work: Maximizing Your Psychological Capital for Success" Wiley, 2010.

17   https://www.youtube.com/watch?v=8yjGPgs0_S0

18   The Mind Unleashed - "The Conscious, Unconscious, and Unconscious Mind – How Does It All Work?" - https://themindunleashed.com/2014/03/conscious-subconscious-unconscious-mind-work.html

19   Psychology Today - "Is Stress Killing Your Relationship? Why You're Not Alone." - https://www.psychologytoday.com/us/blog/between-you-and-me/201709/is-stress-killing-your-relationship-why-youre-not-alone

20   Byrne, R. - "The Magic Secret" - https://www.amazon.com/Magic-Secret-Rhonda-Byrne/dp/1451673442

21   Merrill, D. - "Why Multitasking Doesn't Work" - https://www.forbes.com/sites/douglasmerrill/2012/08/17/why-multitasking-doesnt-work/

22   Francis, T. and Herman, T. - "The Real Cost of Context Switching" - https://www.forbes.com/sites/timfrancis/2017/06/12/the-real-cost-of-context-switching/

23   Bright, D. - "How to Let Go at the End of the Workday" - https://hbr.org/2017/11/how-to-let-go-at-the-end-of-the-workday

24   Clear, J. - "This 100-Year-Old To-Do List Hack Still Works Like A Charm" - https://www.fastcompany.com/3062946/this-100-year-old-to-do-list-hack-still-works-like-a-charm

25   Heid, M. - "This Simple Trick Will Make You Happier and Better at Your Job" - http://amp.timeinc.net/time/5339600/how-to-be-happier-at-work

26   Bradberry, T. - "The Antidote to Stress is Structure" - https://www.linkedin.com/pulse/antidote-stress-structure-dr-travis-bradberry/

27   Walton, A. - "The Pressure Of Answering Work Emails At Night Takes Toll On Mental Health, Study Finds" - https://www-forbes-com.cdn.ampproject.org/c/s/www.forbes.com/sites/alicegwalton/2018/08/10/the-pressure-of-answering-work-emails-at-night-takes-toll-on-mental-health-study-finds/amp

28   Bradberry, T. - "The Antidote to Stress Is Structure" - https://www.linkedin.com/pulse/antidote-stress-structure-dr-travis-bradberry/

29   Acuff, J. - "To Be Good at One Thing You Have to Be Bad at Something Else" - https://www.linkedin.com/pulse/good-one-thing-you-have-bad-something-else-jon-acuff/

30   Segal, J. et al - "Stress in the Workplace - Managing Job and Work Stress" - https://www.helpguide.org/articles/stress/stress-in-the-workplace.htm

31   Kwon, J. - "The Cure for Imposter Syndrome is to Admit You Are Right" - https://www.linkedin.com/pulse/cure-imposter-syndrome-admit-you-right-joe-kwon/

32 Treadwell, D. and Alexander, P. - "Money Isn't All That Matters" - https://www.amazon.com/Money-Isnt-All-That-Matters/dp/0967832101/

33 Abed, R. - "This 1 Question Will Help You Determine If You Should Quit Your Job" - https://www.inc.com/robbie-abed/this-1-question-will-help-you-determine-if-you-should-quit-your-job.html

34 https://www.thejobnetwork.com/how-to-figure-out-if-you-should-quit-your-job-infographic/

35 Inquirer.net - "What is 'ikigai' and How Could It Help You Boost Your Well-Being?" - http://www.thejakartapost.com/life/2018/03/15/what-is-ikigai-and-how-could-it-help-you-boost-your-well-being.html

36 https://theyogahub.ie/ikigai-really-want/

37 Hansen, R. - "The Five-Step Plan for Creating Personal Mission Statements" - https://www.livecareer.com/career/advice/jobs/creating-personal-mission-statements

38 https://www.urbandictionary.com/define.php?term=Passion

39 Khazan, O. - "Find Your Passion Is Awful Advice" - https://www.theatlantic.com/science/archive/2018/07/find-your-passion-is-terrible-advice/564932/

40 https://www.youtube.com/watch?v=tDx4rxXJNYE

41 Robin, V. and Dominguez, J. - "Your Money or Your Life" - https://www.amazon.com/Your-Money-Life-Transforming-Relationship/dp/0143115766/

42 Pasricha, N. - "The Happiness Equation" - https://www.amazon.com/Happiness-Equation-Nothing-Anything-Everything/dp/0425277984/

43 Melnick, S. - "Success Under Stress: Powerful Tools for Staying Calm, Confident, and Productive When the Pressure's On" - pg. 22 - https://www.amazon.com/Success-Under-Stress-Confident-Productive-ebook/dp/B00AG40USW/

44 Alpert, J. - "6 Powerful Ways to Worry Less and Live More" - https://thriveglobal.com/stories/6-powerful-ways-to-worry-less-and-live-more-3/

45 Matheson, M. - "The Church of Failure" - https://www.youtube.com/watch?v=qI9cGJ01ERk

46 Kessels, E. - "Failed It!: How to turn mistakes into ideas and other advice for successfully screwing up" - https://www.amazon.com/Failed-mistakes-advice-successfully-screwing/dp/0714871192/

47 Hu, J. - "Celebrate your failures at Fuckup Nights" - https://qz.com/work/1491752/entrepreneurs-celebrate-their-failures-at-fuckup-nights/

48 Wells, D.L. - "The Effect of Videotapes of Animals on Cardiovascular Responses to Stress" - https://www.researchgate.net/publication/230139763_The_effect_of_videotapes_of_animals_on_cardiovascular_responses_to_stress

[49] Saxon, J. - "Why Your Customers' Attention is the Scarcest Resource in 2017" - https://www.ama.org/partners/content/Pages/why-customers-attention-scarcest-resources-2017.aspx

[50] Edberg, H. - "How to Deal with Stress: 33 Tips That Work" - https://www.positivityblog.com/how-to-deal-with-stress/

[51] Moore, M. - "How To Declipse (Transform) Your Stress" - https://instituteofcoaching.org/blogs/how-declipse-transform-your-stress

[52] Speca, M.; Carlson, L.; Goodey, E. and Angen, M. - "A Randomized, Wait-List Controlled Clinical Trial: The Effect of a Mindfulness Meditation-Based Stress Reduction Program on Mood and Symptoms of Stress in Cancer Outpatients" - https://journals.lww.com/psychosomaticmedicine/Abstract/2000/09000/A_Randomized,_Wait_List_Controlled_Clinical_Trial_.4.aspx

[53] Comstock, J. - "Mindfulness App Measurably Reduces Stress Levels in Small Study" - https://www.mobihealthnews.com/content/mindfulness-app-measurably-reduces-stress-levels-small-study

[54] Power of Positivity - "How to Meditate: Everything You Need to Know to Start Meditation" - https://www.powerofpositivity.com/how-to-meditate-everything-you-need-to-know/

[55] Thrive Global - "Mental Resiliency: Letting Go of the Guilt of Not Getting Things Done" - https://www.thriveglobal.com/stories/mental-resiliency-letting-go-of-the-guilt-of-not-getting-things-done/

[56] Manson, M. - "The Subtle Art of Not Giving a F*ck" - https://www.amazon.com/Subtle-Art-Not-Giving-Counterintuitive/dp/0062457713/

[57] Goldstein, E. - "Stressing Out? S.T.O.P." - https://www.mindful.org/stressing-out-stop/

[58] Alpert, J. - "6 Powerful Ways to Worry Less and Live More" - https://www.thriveglobal.com/stories/34563-6-powerful-ways-to-worry-less-and-live-more

[59] Scott, E. - "The Benefits of Journaling for Stress Management" - https://www.verywellmind.com/the-benefits-of-journaling-for-stress-management-3144611

[60] EurekAlert! - "Writing About Worries Eases Anxiety and Improves Test Performance" - https://www.eurekalert.org/pub_releases/2011-01/uoc-waw011011.php

[61] Alpert, J. - "6 Powerful Ways to Worry Less and Live More" - https://www.thriveglobal.com/stories/34563-6-powerful-ways-to-worry-less-and-live-more

[62] Power of Positivity - "Psychologists Explain How Adult Coloring Is the Best Alternative to Meditation" - https://www.powerofpositivity.com/best-alternative-to-meditation/

63 Carlson, R. - "Don't Sweat the Small Stuff . . . and It's All Small Stuff" - https://www.amazon.com/Dont-Sweat-Small-Stuff-Its/dp/0786881852/

64 Madill, E. - "Why Loving Your Life Is Easier Than You May Think" - https://thriveglobal.com/stories/why-loving-your-life-is-easier-than-you-may-think/

65 Bradberry, T. - "Nine Traps You Fall Into That Limit Your Happiness" - https://www.linkedin.com/pulse/nine-traps-you-fall-limit-your-happiness-dr-travis-bradberry/

66 Hyatt, M. & Harkavy, D. - "Living Forward: A Proven Plan to Stop Drifting and Get the Life You Want" - https://www.amazon.com/exec/obidos/ASIN/080101882X/mhyatt-20

67 Petrie, N. - "Pressure Doesn't Have to Turn into Stress" - https://hbr.org/2017/03/pressure-doesnt-have-to-turn-into-stress

68 Paul, A.M. - "The Secret to Grace Under Pressure" - http://ideas.time.com/2012/03/28/the-secret-to-grace-under-pressure/

69 Firestone, L. - "4 Ways to Overcome Your Inner Critic" - https://www.psychologytoday.com/us/blog/compassion-matters/201305/4-ways-overcome-your-inner-critic

70 Wilding, M. - "Forget Positive Thinking. This Is How to Actually Change Negative Thoughts" - https://medium.com/personal-growth/forget-positive-thinking-this-is-how-to-actually-change-negative-thoughts-2e8126bf7e16

71 Clark, B. - "Is F.E.A.R. Holding You Back?" - https://www.copyblogger.com/f-e-a-r/

72 Robert Schuller, American Pastor and Author, 1926 - 2015.

73 Frances, K. – "The Funny Thing About Stress; a Seriously Humorous Guide to a Happier Life" - https://www.amazon.com/Funny-Stress-Seriously-Humorous-Happier/dp/0984580603/

74 Adult Children of Alcoholics World Service Organization - "The Solution" - https://adultchildren.org/literature/solution/

75 Hartley, R. - "Why the Best Hire Might Not Have the Perfect Resume" - https://youtu.be/jiDQDLnEXdA

76 Sivers, D. - "Anything You Want" - https://www.amazon.com/Anything-You-Want-Lessons-Entrepreneur/dp/1591848261

77 Rock, D. - "Your Brain at Work: Strategies for Overcoming Distraction, Regaining Focus, and Working Smarter All Day Long" - https://www.amazon.com/gp/product/0061771295/

78 James, M. - "Sleep, Cycles and Rebooting Your Brain with Meditation" - https://www.psychologytoday.com/us/blog/focus-forgiveness/201112/sleep-cycles-and-rebooting-your-brain-meditation

79 Lyubomirsky, S. - "The How of Happiness: A New Approach to Getting the Life You Want" - https://www.amazon.com/gp/product/B0010O927W/

80 Barber, E. - "The 5 Habits That Will Make You Happy, According to Science" - http://time.com/4149478/happiness-neuroscience-simplicity/

81 Angel, B. - "Feeling Stuck? Change This One Simple Thing to Refocus Your Mindset." - https://apple.news/AHa3fa-4MMmG1s380WVKDtg

82 Speca, M.; Carlson, L.; Goodey, E. and Angen, M. - "A Randomized, Wait-List Controlled Clinical Trial: The Effect of a Mindfulness Meditation-Based Stress Reduction Program on Mood and Symptoms of Stress in Cancer Outpatients" - https://journals.lww.com/psychosomaticmedicine/Abstract/2000/09000/A_Randomized,_Wait_List_Controlled_Clinical_Trial_.4.aspx

83 Yates, B. - "About Emotional Freedom Techniques® — EFT" - http://www.bradyates.net/eft.html

84 Urban, H. - "Life's Greatest Lessons: 20 Things That Matter" - https://www.amazon.com/Lifes-Greatest-Lessons-Things-Matter/dp/074323782X/

85 Copeland, B. - "SMART Goals - How to Make Your Goals Achievable" - https://www.mindtools.com/pages/article/smart-goals.htm

86 Winfrey, O. - "Oprah's Forgiveness Aha! Moment" - https://www.youtube.com/watch?v=Rwcp_oEIwnU

87 GP Strategies - "Managing Professional Growth" - https://www.gpstrategies.com/solution/organization-leadership-development/employee-engagement/managing-professional-growth/

88 MindTools.com - "What Are Your Values? Deciding What's Most Important in Life" - https://www.mindtools.com/pages/article/newTED_85.htm

89 Imber, A. - "4 Science-Backed Ways to End Your Workday More Successfully" - https://www.businessinsider.com.au/how-to-end-work-more-successfully-2018-9/amp

90 James, M. - "Mental and Emotional Release" - https://www.amazon.com/Mental-Emotional-Release-Matt-James/dp/1504384504/

91 Hansen, P. - "Pathway to Transformation" - http://www.philinthecircle.com/pdf

92 Alpert, J. - "6 Powerful Ways to Worry Less and Live More" - https://thriveglobal.com/stories/6-powerful-ways-to-worry-less-and-live-more-3/

93 Power of Positivity - "5 Scientifically Proven Breathing Techniques For Stress and Anxiety" - https://www.powerofpositivity.com/breathing-techniques-stress-and-anxiety/

94 Khajuria, K. - "Laughter Is the Best Medicine" - http://www.psychiatrictimes.com/cultural-psychiatry/laughter-best-medicine

95 Laughter Yoga - "Curious About Laughter Yoga" - https://laughteryoga.org/laughter-yoga/about-laughter-yoga/

96 Ervolino, B. - "Everybody Is Exhausted: Stress and Social Media are Taking Their Toll" - https://www-chicagotribune-com.cdn.ampproject.org/c/s/

www.chicagotribune.com/lifestyles/health/ct-social-media-exhaustion-20171019-story,amp.html

[97] Krause, E. et al - "Hydration State Controls Stress Responsiveness and Social Behavior" - http://www.jneurosci.org/content/31/14/5470

[98] Gutman, R. - "Smile: The Astonishing Powers of a Simple Act" - https://www.amazon.com/gp/product/B006IS4WW0/

[99] Mann, H. - "I Stopped Drinking Alcohol Over 6 Months Ago and This is What Happened." - https://medium.com/@Harpinder.Mann/i-stopped-drinking-alcohol-over-6-months-ago-and-this-is-what-happened-d57e188791c8

[100] Magee, E. - "Health by Chocolate" - https://www.webmd.com/diet/features/health-by-chocolate

[101] Physiology & Behavior - "Chewing Gum Alleviates Negative Mood and Reduces Cortisol During Acute Laboratory Psychological Stress" - Volume 97, Issues 3-4, 22 June 2009, Pages 304-312

[102] Nishigaki, H. - "How to Good-bye Depression" - https://www.amazon.com/How-Good-bye-Depression-Constrict-Everyday/dp/0595094724/

[103] Sonnenberg, A. - "5 Tips to Managing Daily Stress" - https://www.activebeat.com/fitness/5-tips-to-managing-daily-stress/4/

[104] Rundle, A. - "Just How Bad Is Business Travel for Your Health? Here's the Data." - https://hbr.org/2018/05/just-how-bad-is-business-travel-for-your-health-heres-the-data

[105] Zinczenko, D. - "Eat This Not That! Restaurant Survival Guide: The No-Diet Weight Loss Solution" - https://www.amazon.com/This-That-Restaurant-Survival-Guide/dp/160529540X/

[106] Biol Psychol. - "Blood Pressure Reactivity to Stress is Better for People who Recently had Penile-Vaginal Intercourse than for People who had Other or No Sexual Activity." 2006 Feb;71(2):214-22. Epub 2005 Jun 14.

[107] Santas, D. - "Six Mind-Body Tips for Less Holiday Stress" - https://amp-cnn-com.cdn.ampproject.org/c/s/amp.cnn.com/cnn/2017/12/20/health/mind-body-holiday-stress-tips-santas/index.html

[108] Mayo Clinic - "Exercise and Stress: Get Moving to Manage Stress" - https://www.mayoclinic.org/healthy-lifestyle/stress-management/in-depth/exercise-and-stress/art-20044469

[109] Santas, D. - "Six Mind-Body Tips for Less Holiday Stress" - https://amp-cnn-com.cdn.ampproject.org/c/s/amp.cnn.com/cnn/2017/12/20/health/mind-body-holiday-stress-tips-santas/index.html

[110] Elkhaim, Y. - "The Truth About How Much Water You Should Really Drink" - https://health.usnews.com/health-news/blogs/eat-run/2013/09/13/the-truth-about-how-much-water-you-should-really-drink

111 Jarrett, C. - "An Afternoon Nap Tunes Out Negative Emotions, Tunes In Positive Ones" - https://bps-research-digest.blogspot.com/2011/03/afternoon-nap-tunes-out-negative.html

112 Van Edwards, V. - "The Science of Napping: Ideal Nap Lengths and the Perfect Time" - https://www.scienceofpeople.com/science-perfect-nap/

113 Ober, C., Chevalier, G. and Zucker, M. - "Grounding the Human Body: The Healing Benefits of Earthing" - https://chopra.com/articles/grounding-the-human-body-the-healing-benefits-of-earthing

114 https://traumaprevention.com/

115 Berceli, D. - "Trauma Releasing Exercises" - https://www.amazon.com/Trauma-Releasing-Exercises-David-Berceli-ebook/dp/B004S2CC7K/

116 Berceli, D. - "Trauma Releasing Exercises Step By Step Video Instruction and Demonstration" - https://www.amazon.com/Trauma-Releasing-Exercises-Instruction-Demonstration/dp/B001XI23E4/

117 https://traumaprevention.com/event/categories/workshops/

118 National Sleep Foundation - "What Is Good Quality Sleep?" - https://www.sleepfoundation.org/press-release/what-good-quality-sleep

119 Bradberry, T. - "The Antidote to Stress is Structure" - https://www.linkedin.com/pulse/antidote-stress-structure-dr-travis-bradberry/

120 Treadwell, D. and Alexander, P. - "Money Isn't All That Matters" - https://www.amazon.com/Money-Isnt-All-That-Matters/dp/0967832101/

121 Spector, J. - "How I Stopped Working So Much and What I Learned From Doing So" - https://medium.com/an-idea-for-you/how-i-stopped-working-so-much-and-what-i-learned-from-it-16e7c76a0519

122 Hover, G. - "My New Year's Resolution: Stop Being Busy" - https://www.linkedin.com/pulse/my-new-years-resolution-stop-being-busy-gretchen-hover/

123 The Coaching Tools Company - "De-Stress Series: 10 Easy Ways to Help Your Clients (and You!) Find The Calm You Need" - https://www.thecoachingtoolscompany.com/de-stress-tips-series-10-ways-to-find-the-calm-you-need/

124 Rubin, G. - "Happier at Home: Kiss More, Jump More, Abandon Self-Control, and My Other Experiments in Everyday Life" - https://www.amazon.com/Happier-Home-Self-Control-Experiments-Everyday/dp/0307886794/

125 Perlow, L. - "Stop the Meeting Madness" - https://hbr.org/2017/07/stop-the-meeting-madness

126 Peláez, M. - "Plan Your Way to Less Stress, More Happiness" - http://healthland.time.com/2011/05/31/study-25-of-happiness-depends-on-stress-management/

127 Davidson, S.G. - "101 Ways to Have a Great Day at Work" - https://www.amazon.com/101-Ways-Have-Great-Work/dp/1402207794/

128 Edberg, H. - "How to Deal with Stress: 33 Tips That Work" - https://www.positivityblog.com/how-to-deal-with-stress/

129 Wong, K. - "How To Worry Better" - https://www.thecut.com/2017/11/how-to-be-better-at-worrying.html

130 Edberg, H. - "How to Deal with Stress: 33 Tips That Work" - https://www.positivityblog.com/how-to-deal-with-stress/

131 Bradberry, T. - "The Antidote to Stress is Structure" - https://www.linkedin.com/pulse/antidote-stress-structure-dr-travis-bradberry/

132 Boyes, A. - "5 Things to Do When You Feel Overwhelmed by Your Workload" - https://hbr.org/2018/08/5-things-to-do-when-you-feel-overwhelmed-by-your-workload

133 James, G. - "It's Official: Open Plan Offices Are Now the Dumbest Management Fad of All Time" - https://www.inc.com/geoffrey-james/its-official-open-plan-offices-are-now-dumbest-management-fad-of-all-time.html

134 https://www.amazon.com/Dammit-Doll-Ménage-Random-Stress/dp/B00G05DYTI/

135 Barking Up The Wrong Tree - "How To Quickly And Easily Reduce Anxiety" - https://www.bakadesuyo.com/2011/02/how-to-quickly-and-easily-reduce-anxiety/

136 Red Rain Buddha - "5 Reasons Why You Need A Desktop Zen Garden" - https://redrainbuddhastore.com/blogs/news/5-reasons-why-you-need-a-desktop-zen-garden

137 Amodeo, J. - "Are You Suffering from News Exposure Stress Syndrome?" - https://www.psychologytoday.com/us/blog/intimacy-path-toward-spirituality/201804/are-you-suffering-news-exposure-stress-syndrome

138 https://www.magictricks.com/pride-and-joy-card.html

139 Social Science & Medicine - "Green Space as a Buffer Between Stressful Life Events and Health" - Volume 70, Issue 8, April 2010, Pages 1203-1210

140 Agarwal, P. - "How Do We Design Workplaces That Support Mental Health And Well-Being" - https://www.forbes.com/sites/pragyaagarwaleurope/2018/06/24/how-can-workplace-design-help-mental-health/

141 Lee, S. - "Why Indoor Plants Make You Feel Better" - https://www.nbcnews.com/better/health/indoor-plants-can-instantly-boost-your-health-happiness-ncna781806

142 Ervolino, B. "Everybody Is Exhausted: Stress And Social Media Are Taking Their Toll" - https://www-chicagotribune-com.cdn.approject.org/c/s/www.chicagotribune.com/lifestyles/health/ct-social-media-exhaustion-20171019-story.amp.html

143 Bradberry, T. - "The Antidote to Stress is Structure" - https://www.linkedin.com/pulse/antidote-stress-structure-dr-travis-bradberry/

144 Parker-Pope, T. - "How to Be Happy" - https://www.nytimes.com/guides/well/how-to-be-happy

145 Brickel, R. - "Healthy Relationships Matter More Than We Think" -
https://pro.psychcentral.com/healthy-relationships-matter-more-than-we-think/

146 Bradberry, T. – "Stress Literally Shrinks Your Brain (How to Reverse
the Damage)" - https://www.govexec.com/excellence/promising-
practices/2015/12/stress-literally-shrinks-your-brain-how-reverse-
damage/124626/

147 Fowler, J. & Christakis, N. - "Dynamic Spread Of Happiness In A Large Social
Network: Longitudinal Analysis Over 20 years In The Framingham Heart
Study" - https://www.bmj.com/content/337/bmj.a2338.full

148 Barker, E. - "New Neuroscience Reveals 4 Rituals That Will Make You
Happy" - https://www.theladders.com/career-advice/neuroscience-4-rituals-
happy

149 Olson, J. - "The Slight Edge: Turning Simple Disciplines into Massive
Success and Happiness" - https://www.amazon.com/Slight-Edge-Turning-
Disciplines-Happiness/dp/1626340463/

150 Barker, E. - "Silicon Valley's Best Networker Teaches You His Secrets" -
https://www.bakadesuyo.com/2013/02/interview-silicon-valleys-networker-
teaches-secrets-making-connections/

151 Journal of Experimental Social Psychology - "Is Compassion for Others
Stress Buffering? Consequences of Compassion and Social Support for
Physiological Reactivity to Stress" - Volume 46, Issue 5, September 2010,
Pages 816-823

152 Wiest, B. - "18 Things You Need to Give Up to Become a High-Achieving
Person" - https://www.forbes.com/sites/briannawiest/2018/03/20/18-
things-you-need-to-give-up-to-become-a-high-achieving-
person/#76400a5011fa

153 Goudreau, J. - "12 Ways to Eliminate Stress at Work" - https://www.forbes.com
/sites/jennagoudreau/2013/03/20/12-ways-to-eliminate-stress-at-
work/#3738097e7f29

154 Hall, J. - "7 Productivity Habits That Will Make You a More Helpful Person"
- https://www-forbes-com.cdn.ampproject.org/c/s/www.forbes.com/sites/
johnhall/2018/08/12/7-productivity-habits-that-will-make-you-a-more-
helpful-person/amp/

155 Bradberry, T. – "Stress Literally Shrinks Your Brain (How to Reverse
the Damage)" - https://www.govexec.com/excellence/promising-
practices/2015/12/stress-literally-shrinks-your-brain-how-reverse-
damage/124626/

156 James, M. - "Ho'oponopono: Your Path to True Forgiveness" -
https://www.amazon.com/Hooponopono-Your-Path-True-Forgiveness/
dp/1944177795

157 White, M.G. - "Positive Strategies in Managing Stress" -
https://stress.lovetoknow.com/Positive_Strategies_in_Managing_Stress

158 https://www.linkedin.com/in/tracy-appleton-lcsw-med-6531b534/

159 The Trusted Advisor - "The Trust Equation" - https://trustedadvisor.com/
why-trust-matters/understanding-trust/understanding-the-trust-equation

160 Schwantes, M. - "Want to Improve Your Life Instantaneously? Try These
7 Simple Habits (1 Habit per Day for 1 Week)" - https://www.inc.com/
marcel-schwantes/7-ways-to-dramatically-improve-your-life-in-7-days-
starting-this-week.html

161 Carucci, R. – "Stress Leads to Bad Decisions. Here's How to Avoid Them"
- https://hbr.org/2017/08/stress-leads-to-bad-decisions-heres-how-to-avoid-
them

162 Carucci, R. – "Stress Leads to Bad Decisions. Here's How to Avoid Them"
- https://hbr.org/2017/08/stress-leads-to-bad-decisions-heres-how-to-avoid-
them

163 Campbell, S. - "6 Simple Ways to Manage and Overcome Stress" -
https://www-entrepreneur-com.cdn.ampproject.org/c/s/www.entrepreneur.com
/amphtml/315321

164 Science Daily - "Membership in Many Groups Leads to Quick
Recovery from Physical Challenges" - https://www.sciencedaily.com/
releases/2010/12/101215141921.htm

165 Power of Positivity - "7 Good Things That Will Happen If You Have A Stress
Free Home" - https://www.powerofpositivity.com/good-things-happen-in-
a-stress-free-home/

Made in the USA
Las Vegas, NV
25 May 2022

49357578R00134